THE BOOK ON DATA STRUCTURES

THE BOOK ON DATA STRUCTURES

VOLUME I

Authored by:
David R. Richardson

Edited by:
Jennifer Elaine Estock
Thomas J. Limber III

Writers Club Press
San Jose New York Lincoln Shanghai

The Book on Data Structures
Volume I

Writers Club Press
an imprint of iUniverse, Inc.

For information address:
iUniverse, Inc.
5220 S. 16th St., Suite 200
Lincoln, NE 68512
www.iuniverse.com

ISBN: 0-595-24039-9

Printed in the United States of America

I would like to dedicate this book to my dearest Jeni. Without her constant love and support, this book would have not have been possible.

CONTENTS

NOTES ON ARITHMETIC OPERATORS USED IN THIS BOOK:

Representations of arithmetic operators used in this book are reflections of arithmetic operators you will see used in text files and documents you will find on the internet.

Because it is not always convenient to use standard arithmetic operators when composing a document (e-mail, ASCII text, etc), a de facto standard appeared among computer users over time to represent arithmetic operators. I will list the operators you will find in this text (and many others) along with their usage.

Operation	Operator	Example
Addition	+	40 + 2
Subtraction	-	44–2
Multiplication	*	6 * 7
Multiplication	x	6 x 7
Division	\	84 \ 2
Division	/	21 / 0.5
Exponent	^	6 ^ 2.086033
Exponent	**	6**2.086033

You will see the second division operator(\)less frequently than the first(/).

The second multiplication operator (x) is rarely used.

The exponent operators can be read as "to the power of" so if you were to see 10^5 you would read the statement as "ten to the power of 5".

The second exponent operator (**) doesn't seem to make much sense. It appeared as an operator originally for representing exponents in FORTRAN. It is rarely used, but appears in enough places to warrant a listing here.

You will also see, on occasion, SQR() and LOG() used in arithmetic opera-tions. The SQR() is used to show that we are taking the square root of the result of the operation that is shown between the parentheses. (i.e. SQR(100) would equal 10) the LOG() is used in the same manner, there is a difference, however. If you see LOG(N) we will assume that we are returning the natural logarithm of N. If you see LOG10(N) we are taking the base 10 logarithm of N. The 10, in this case, is the number base. It can be replaced with any num-ber base that is needed for the application.

INTRODUCTION

DATA AND STRUCTURE

All computer programs use data in some way. Some programs simply generate data needing no input. Some programs produce data given a set of input data. And some programs simply manipulate data given a data set.

The study of data structures is the study of data organization, data storage, and the relationship among data sets. A data set's structure determines how efficiently information is stored, retrieved, or modified.

The study of data structures is not limited to the study of groups of data sets. The study of data structures also extends to the study of the representation of individual data elements. This includes how different types of data are represented in a computer's memory in the seemingly simply binary number system.

The study of data structures also includes the study of operations performed on the structure itself. This includes sorting the data and search the data, among other things.

It is also important to study the implementation of a data structure. That is, how a data structure is built for use in a computer program. The study of implementation is important as it can give you valuable insight into how a specific data structure works to manage your data. This knowledge is particularly important when choosing a data structure for a certain application.

Scalar Variable Types

A scalar variable type is one that defines a single data element, or variable. Each programming language may contain different types of scalar variables, however, there is set of types that are common to most modern programming languages. This set includes Integers, Floating point numbers, Characters, and Boolean type variables. You will also see variations of these types, including Long integers, and double or single precision Floating point numbers that are also very common among modern programming languages.

Aggregate Structures

Scalar variables are useful for solving many problems involving data storage. However, they do have their limitations. If you desired to store a list of numbers, you would have to define a variable for each number. When dealing with large amounts of data, this can become tedious and inefficient. To overcome these inherent limitations, Aggregate structures are used. An aggregate structure is used to store a group of scalar variables under a single name.

Aggregate structures solve many problems, including the storage text, lists of numbers, and lists of related data. The two most common aggregate structures include the Array and the Record. Each will be reviewed in detail in chapter 3.

Abstract Data Types

There are some data structures that a particular programming language may implement inherently, such as arrays. However, many of the data structures that you will use in a computer program are simply abstractions of the types that are already available.

These types of data structures are abstract because their definition is primarily defined by their usage. For example, a stack is an abstract data type that can be created using an array and an integer. The type is considered abstract, because there is no actual stack type, it is simply a way to use an integer and an array together

An abstract data type will provide a very clear distinction between how we view the structure of the data, and the actual way that the data is represented in memory. In this way, by using abstract data types, we can represent very complex data sets in a simple manner. This leads to fewer errors in the program that the structure is implemented in, and less work for the programmer after the structure, and its interface, are implemented.

Because abstract data types are so important, many programming languages have added extra support for their creation and usage. In fact, in some programming languages, you can abstract an abstract data type to the point that its use appears as seemless as the use of a scalar variable type.

Many object oriented programming languages let you take this a step further and allow you to define how certain operations are preformed on your data structure. For example, if you created a Fraction data type that simply holds 2 integers (for numerator and denominator) you could decide how the addition (+) operator managed the addition of two variables of your Fraction type. (Note that the computer could not understand how to use your type in such an operation without this definition.)

1

Number representations
Introduction

Digital computer systems manipulate data in a Base 2 or Binary form. A single binary digit is called a bit. Bits may have only one of 2 values, 0 or 1. There systems can form larger numbers by grouping collections of these single binary digits.

Alien Bases

It is not always convenient for a human operator to view or manage data in binary form. Although there are times when it is necessary, it is often more convenient to work with numbers represented in a different base. The three most common ways that binary data is represented are base 8 (octal), base 10 (decimal), and base 16 (hexadecimal). Any power of 2 is equally as effective as 8 and 16, however, these other bases have never been used in the mainstream.

To avoid any confusion as to how numbers are represented in this chapter, I will mark all numbers with a letter corresponding to their base. (i.e. h for hex, d for decimal, etc.) It is traditional to use a subscript to represent a numbers base, however, I've found that is less confusing to someone reading a text to represent a numbers base in the aforementioned way.

Before we continue into the details of each number base, we should first consider how a number system uses place value. A digit's value, in an arbitrary base, can be calculated by multiplying the digit's magnitude by its base raised to the power of its position. The value of the whole number is the sum of the value of all its digits. For example: 256d = (6 x 10^0) + (5 x 10^1) + (2 x 10^2) = (6 x 1) + (5 x 10) + (2 x 100) = 6 + 50 + 200 = 256d.

We can do the same thing with the binary number 1010b.

0x2^0 = 0
1x2^1 = 2
0x2^2 = 0
1x2^3 = 8
0 + 2 + 0 + 8 = 10d

Or, alternately, on a number in base 8: 673o.

3x8^0 = 3
7x8^1 = 56
6x8^2 = 384
3 + 56 + 384 = 443d

From the examples, you can see that a numbers place value relates, simply, to how many groups of b^n have been accounted for. In the number 256d, for example, we have two groups of 100 (10^2), five groups of 10 (10^1), and six groups of 1 (10^0). Quite simply, a numbers base defines what these groups will be. This makes counting in any number base very simple as you need only begin a new, or increment, a group when you complete a cycle through each symbol in that group's predecessor.

To count in Hexadecimal (base 16):

0, 1, 2, 3, 4, 5, 6, 7, 8, 9, A, B, C, D, E, F, 10, 11, 12, …, 1A, 1B, 1C, 1D, 1E, 1F, 20, 21, 22

In the last number we counted to, 22h, we have 2 groups of 16 and 2 groups of 1 or 34d.

Or, alternately, to count in Binary (base 2):

0, 1, 10, 11, 100, 101, 110, 111, 1000, 1001, 1010, 1011, 1100, 1101, 1110, 1111

In the last number we counted to, 1111b, we have 1 group of 8, 1 group of 4, 1 group of 2, and 1 group of 1 or 15d.

Base Conversion

It is important for the computer scientist to be able to convert numbers between bases almost automatically. It is particularly important to be able to convert between binary and decimal, hexadecimal and decimal, and binary and hexadecimal. It is becoming less important every year to be able to convert numbers to and from octal, however, it is important to cover the number base for purposes of completeness and clarity.

The following table shows the numbers 0–15 shows their equivalency in different number bases. Committing this table to memory will be invaluable.

Binary	Octal	Decimal	Hexadecimal
0	0	0	0
1	1	1	1
10	2	2	2
11	3	3	3
100	4	4	4
101	5	5	5
110	6	6	6
111	7	7	7
1000	10	8	8
1001	11	9	9
1010	12	10	A
1011	13	11	B
1100	14	12	C

Binary	Octal	Decimal	Hexadecimal
1101	15	13	D
1110	16	14	E
1111	17	15	F

Conversion from decimal (base 10) to binary (base 2):

To convert a number from decimal to binary, divide the number by 2, save the remainder, and continue dividing the result by 2 until the result is 0.

Example: 23d to binary

23 / 2 = 11 with a remainder of 1
11 / 2 = 5 with a remainder of 1
5 / 2 = 2 with a remainder of 1
2 / 2 = 1 with a remainder of 0
1 / 2 = 0 with a remainder of 1

The results in order of least significance: 10111b = 23d
To show that 10111b is indeed 23d calculate the value of 10111b as shown in the previous section:

$1x2^0 = 1$
$1x2^1 = 2$
$1x2^2 = 4$
$0x2^3 = 0$
$1x2^4 = 16$
$1 + 2 + 4 + 0 + 16 = 23d$

Conversion from decimal (base 10) to octal (base 8):

To convert a number from decimal to octal, divide the number by 8, save the remainder, and continue dividing the result by 8 until the result is 0.

Example: 42d to octal

42 / 8 = 5 with a remainder of 2

5 / 8 = 0 with a remainder of 5

The results in order of least significance: 52o = 42d

To show that 52o is indeed 42d calculate the value of 52o as shown in the previous section:

$2x8^0 = 2$

$5x8^1 = 40$

$2 + 40 = 42d$

Conversion from decimal (base 10) to hexadecimal (base 16):

To convert a number from base 10 to base 16, first convert the number from base 10 to base 2. Then divide the resulting binary number into quartets (groups of 4 bits) and convert each 4 bit binary number to its hexadecimal equivalent by either looking its equivalency up in the chart show at the beginning of this section or, alternately, by converting each quartet into base 10 and replacing any resulting 2 digit decimal number with its hexadecimal equivalent (10 = A, 11 = B, etc).

Example: Convert the decimal (base 10) number 93d to Hexadecimal (base 16):

93 / 2 = 46 with a remainder of 1

46 / 2 = 23 with a remainder of 0

23 / 2 = 11 with a remainder of 1

11 / 2 = 5 with a remainder of 1

5 / 2 = 2 with a remainder of 1

2 / 2 = 1 with a remainder of 0

1 / 2 = 0 with a remainder of 1

187d = 1011101b

Append zeros to the most significant end of the resulting number so that the number of digits is evenly divisible by 4.

1011101b = 01011101b

Now divide the resulting binary number into quartets, or "nibbles".

[0101] [1101]

Find the Hexadecimal value of each quartet and replace.

0101b   1101b
5d   13d
5h   Dh

Group the results together in order:

5Dh = 1011101b = 93d

Chapter 1 Exercises

Convert the following binary numbers to base 10:

1) 1011 1001
2) 0010 1101
3) 0110 0110
4) 1001 1001
5) 0101 1011

Convert the following base 16 numbers to base 10:

6) B4
7) 4C
8) CD
9) 21
10) 42

Convert the following base 8 numbers to base 10:

11) 47
12) 14
13) 38
14) 11
15) 10

Convert the following decimal numbers to binary:

16) 58
17) 132
18) 255
19) 128
20) 42

Convert the following base 2 numbers to hexadecimal:

21) 1101 1001
22) 1011 1111
23) 0110 1011
24) 0100 0001
25) 1010 0101

2

Scalar Variables
Computer Memory

Computer memory can be expressed as a long series of pigeonholes, each individually numbered, called memory addresses. Each individual memory location consists of a series of binary (two state) switches that represent bits. The term "bit" is short for binary digit. Each bit can be in a state of on (1) or off (0). By examining the state of the bits in each "pigeon hole" we can determine what number (in base 2) is represented at that memory address. Each memory address is numbered sequentially starting at 0. So if an older computer has 640,000 memory locations then they would be number 0–639,999.

In the old mainframe days of computers, a typical memory location was called a word. A word was typically made up of 8, 16, 32, 40, or 64 bits. In recent years, it is more common to view memory addresses at the byte level (an address for every 8 bits). You will also see a word used more commonly to refer to groups of 2 bytes. The term nibble refers to one half of one byte, or 4 bits.

As personal computers become increasingly powerful, and high-end server computers are simply very powerful equivalents of the personal computer (multiple processors, etc.), we are seeing a move more toward all computers sharing the same basic architecture based more on the personal computer. It is less important today to talk about word sizes, where 20 years ago it was very important. Even powerful super-computers are being replaced in large data processing centers with clusters of small personal computers working in tandem. For the rest of this book we will assume that you are working with a personal computer.

Data Types

There are four data types that are common to most modern programming languages. You may hear them referred to by different names depending on the programming language that they are used in.

Integer	No decimal precision, useful for many applications.
Float	Decimal precision, Used to store floating point numbers (real)
Character	Used to store single letters, numbers, punctuation, etc.
Boolean	Used to story a Boolean value (true or false)

You may also see variations of these types such as Long (an integer type that can store larger numbers) or Double (a float type that can store larger numbers with greater precision) alongside these types. Each programming language can have different names or even implementations of these types. You should consult your programming language's documentation to determine what types it supports.

Data stored in a program can also be classified based on whether or not the value of that data is allowed to be modified. That is dependent on whether the value at that memory address is "Constant'" or not. You may define a variable called pi with a value of 3.141592653589 that is constant, so you cannot accidentally change the value of pi during a program's execution. Technically speaking, if a variable is constant then it is no longer a variable but a constant. It is increasingly common to use the term variable for any memory location. However, if you know a variable is constant, you should refer to it as such.

Because computer memory can only store binary information (numeric data in base 2), all information numeric or non-numeric must be translated into some kind of binary code before storage. This code must be unique to the variables type and easy to manipulate to perform operations such as addition or subtraction. In short, the computer must have some way of determining what type of data is stored at what address so that operations can be pre-formed properly.

In order to overcome this problem, when a program is compiled (converted from human-readable source code, to computer-readable machine code) a symbol table is created in which each variable is listed (by address) alongside its type. In some cases, the variable's initial value is also stored in the symbol table, such as in a language that automatically initializes variables, or in languages that allow you to initialize a variable with a value during its declaration, or when a constant is defined.

The term scalar is used to refer to a variable (or constant) if it is associated with a single memory address. Most variables you will use will be scalar.

Data Encoding
Integers

As stated earlier, when representing an integer, the most significant bit (left-most bit) is used to determine the numbers sign. This bit is referred to as the sign bit. The sign bit can have either a value of 0 for positive numbers, or 1 for negative numbers. The rest of the bits in the number refer to the number's actual value. This is sometimes referred to as the mantissa or magnitude of the number.

One would think that the problem of positive and negative integers would have been completely solved by the use of the sign bit. Unfortunately, this isn't the case at all. If we represent a number in a standard sign/value form when we perform an arithmetic operation we need to determine whether the number's signs are different or the same and use a different algorithm to perform the operation. In addition to this new problem, there are 2 values for 0, a +0 and a -0. This is also problem.

The solution to the first problem is to simply convert the number's value to the ones compliment of itself. This method still requires the use of the sign bit. The ones compliment of the number's value is simply an inversion of the bits in the mantissa. For example: if we took the negative number 10001010 the ones compliment would be: 11110101. With this scheme, the same algorithm can be used no matter what the signs of the numbers are. However, the second problem still exists, there are 2 representations of 0 one positive, and one negative.

The solution, of course, is to find the twos compliment of the magnitude. The twos compliment is formed by first finding the ones compliment of the value and adding 1. Therefore, the number 10000010 would become 11111110 (the ones compliment would have been 11111101). This allows for only one representation of 0 and solves the first problem as well.

It is important to note here that the sign-value, ones compliment, and twos compliment schemes are applicable to both signed and unsigned numbers, however no matter what the scheme any positive numbers remain unchanged from the sign-value scheme. So if you're using the twos compliment scheme you only compliment the value of the negative numbers, leaving the positive numbers alone. Only negative numbers need encoded beyond the sign-value encoding.

Floating-point numbers

Floating-point numbers, also known as real numbers, have been notoriously difficult to represent. For the purposes of this text we will describe the current IEEE standard for representing floating point numbers. You can read more about the standard by reading the IEEE Standard 754-1985.

Floating-point numbers are stored in a form of scientific notation. This allows us to avoid storing a decimal point. For example, if we were to store the number 5.5 we could represent the number as a $55*10^{-1}$. In binary, however, the exponents' base would be 2 instead of 10.

A standard floating-point number is 4 bytes (32 bits) in length. The most significant bit is used as the sign bit and is in the standard form 1 for negative 0 for positive.

The sign bit

[0] 00000000 00000000000000000000000

The next 8 bits are used for the exponent. Instead of using a sign bit to determine whether or not the exponent is positive or negative it uses a bias value of 127 which is added to the exponent that is desired to be expressed in order to guarantee that the number being expressed in always positive. For example, if you wanted to represent the number -45 you would add 127 to the value to guarantee that the exponent is always positive (-45 + 127 = 82).

The exponent

0 [00000000] 00000000000000000000000

The remaining 23 bits are used for the mantissa. The mantissa is sometimes referred to as the fractional part of the floating-point number. There is an implied bit (called the hidden bit) at the most significant position in the mantissa. The bit is not actually there because its value is always 1 and can be assumed.

Remember that the mantissa is the fractional part of the binary number (everything after the decimal point). The digits represent decreasing powers of two, just as in a base 10 number the fractional part (everything after the decimal point) they are in decreasing powers of ten (0.4 is 4 tenths). So 1.1011 in binary represents: 1 whole, 1 half, no quarters, one eighth, and one sixteenth. Because the hidden bit is always one, the visible part of the mantissa starts at one half and continues down. When you calculate the value of the mantissa, be sure to always include 1 whole to account for the hidden bit.

By using this system all real numbers are reduced to fractions. The alert reader will question the accuracy of certain real numbers in such a situation. How can you represent numbers with infinite expansion, such a 1/3 or pi? How do I represent numbers that cannot be expressed in powers of 2, such as 0.4?

Because we have only a finite amount of space to store real numbers, some compromises were made. It was decided that precision was less important than the ability to represent more numbers in the given space. With this system, sometimes when you expect to see the number 0.02 you find the number 0.0200000003 in its place. Some numbers are approximated or truncated to fit within the bounds of allowable space. Until a better system comes along, we have to allow a certain amount of tolerance when dealing with floating point numbers.

You're probably wondering how you can represent the number 0.0 when the hidden bit always refers to 1. Special cases have been defined to allow for 0.0, as it is still a very important number.

There are two ways to define 0.0:

0 00000000 00000000000000000000000
1 00000000 00000000000000000000000

This allows for two possible value for zero, a positive 0.0 and a negative 0.0. However, the IEEE standard states that they will evaluate the same way.

There is another special case. When the exponent part of the number is 00000000 then all the bits in the mantissa must also be 0. If any of the bits in the mantissa are 1 instead of 0 then the number is labeled NaN (Not a Number). This is useful for catching malformed floating-point numbers as well as catching number underflow. Underflow is similar to overflow (where a number grows to large to fit in the space given) except underflow only occurs when a number grows too small to fit in the bounds set by a standard floating point number.

Characters

A Character is simply a group of bits, usually one byte in length that stores a number that relates to a symbol. A symbol could be anything from the letter "a" to the Greek letter sigma. Characters are used to refer to letters, numerals, punctuation marks, bullet points, even arithmetic operators. There are 3 major coding schemes in use.

EBCDIC (Extended Binary Coded Decimal Information Code)—This coding scheme is old and outdated, but is still used in some old IBM mainframe computers. In fact, EBCDIC was originally designed by IBM. Unless you're updating old software on an antiquated IBM mainframe computer, you shouldn't concern yourself with EBCDIC.

ASCII (American Standard Code for Information Interchange)—This is the ANSI standard code used in most personal computers today. Each character is 8 bits, or 1 byte in size and refers to the first 128 characters in the sequence. The rest of the characters are used as extended characters and can change between operating systems. (MS-Dos and Linux have different extended characters, but still follow the ASCII standard).

Unicode—This is an ISO standard designed to act as a unified character-coding scheme. It is designed to represent every character in use by every major language in the world. This includes the Cyrillic characters and many of the characters used in Asian languages. The Unicode standard has been changing frequently, but seems to be settling down.

Boolean values

A Boolean variable can have only two states, true or false. This type derives its name from the famous mathematician George Boole who developed a system of logic that evaluates statements as being either true or false.

Boolean values can be represented in a number of ways. When referring to a single bit, we usually associate 1 with being true and 0 with being false. However, because a single bit is not directly addressable, a Boolean variable will usually occupy an entire byte or more in memory. Many languages refer to a Boolean value as being true if its value is nonzero, and false if the value is zero. Some languages will mask the byte with an AND operation so that the Boolean value is always reduced to either 1 or 0 (i.e. the non-zero value 01101011 masked by performing an AND operation against 00000001 will produce: 00000001 as a result)

Thoughts on Variable Declaration

Declaring a variable gives the computer a chance to allocate space in memory to store that variable's data. It also allows you to specify a variable's type, which is very important.

Many modern programming languages such as LISP and BASIC do not require that you declare a variable before its use—this can lead to problems. In most cases, when you use a variable without first declaring it, the variable it is assigned a default type. If the default type for an undeclared variable is a float type, and you intend to use the variable for integer operations, your program will run slower as floating point operations run slower than integer operations. In short, declaring your variables allows you more control over your program, and gives you a better idea of how your program is using memory.

Other languages (C, C++, Pascal, Java, and many others) require you to declare your variables before use. In such a language, the compiler will throw an error notifying you that an undeclared variable was used. This kind of enforcement allows you to catch many of the errors that undeclared variables may cause before they become a problem.

Thoughts on Variable Types

When an arithmetic operation is performed, a variable's type must be known in order to interpret the value of the variable properly. If the type was unknown, a running program could mistake a four-byte integer for a floating-point number. Because the encoding is different, this could cause an unrecoverable error such as an underflow. (Remember that different variable types are stored differently, or with different encoding, in memory) For this reason, most compilers produce a symbol table that is used to identify a variable's type before any operations are performed on it. This way, when there is a question as to a variable's type, or even length, its type can be easily determined.

Variables of different types, such as integer and float, cannot be used together when an arithmetic operation is performed. To overcome this problem, many computer languages implicitly convert the type of one of the variables to use temporarily during the calculation. Depending on the conversion the compiler will usually produce a warning message to notify you that an implicit conversion is taking place. If you are to assign a value from one variable to another of a different, less precise type, the compiler will warn you that a loss of precision will occur.

Sometimes the compiler chooses to implicitly convert a variable that you didn't intend it to convert. This can lead to many problems, and possibly errors, in your program during execution. To insure that the conversion that you desire to happen is used, it is important to explicitly convert a variable from one type to another. This type of conversion is sometimes called "type casting" as you "cast the type" onto the variable. I would recommend that when you perform any operation on variables of different types that you explicitly cast the variable's type to avoid any potential problems.

Chapter 2 Exercises

1) The term bit is short for _____.

    A) Binary Item
    B) Basic Information Type
    C) Binary Digit
    D) Basic Item Type

2) The Four most common data type are _____, _____, _____, and _____.

3) A data item whose value cannot be changed is called a _____.

    A) Static
    B) Constant
    C) Variable
    D) Literal

4) A data item whose value can be changed is called a _____.

    A) Static
    B) Constant
    C) Variable
    D) Literal

5) A data item that is associated with a single memory address is referred to as _____.

    A) Simple
    B) Constant
    C) Addressable
    D) Scalar

6) The most significant bit in an integer variable is referred to as the _____ bit.

    A) Sign
    B) Last

C) Inversion

D) Flag

Label the following parts of this IEEE 754-1985 Standard Floating Point number:

7) $\boxed{1}$ 11111111   11111111111111111111111

8) 1 $\boxed{11111111}$ 11111111111111111111111

9) 1   11111111 $\boxed{11111111111111111111111}$

Identify the value of the following 2-byte integer variables:

10) 1000 0000 0110 1001

11) 1000 0000 1101 1110

12) 0000 0000 1101 0101

13) 0000 0000 0110 1101

14) 1000 0000 1110 1010

Convert the following IEEE 754-1985 Floating Point Number to a fraction:

15) 0 10000001 10101000000000000000000

Find the ones compliment of the following binary numbers:

16) 1101 1110

17) 0111 1011

18) 0110 1101

19) 1101 1010

20) 1010 0101

Find the twos compliment of the following binary numbers:

21) 1101 1110

22) 0111 1011

23) 0110 1101

24) 1101 1010
25) 1010 0101

3

Arrays and Records
Aggregate Structures

You can see from the previous chapter that there are limitations to what you can do with scalar variable types. If you wanted to keep a list of phone numbers in your program, you would have to define a variable for each number. If you wanted to store the phrase "Hello, World!", you would have to define a variable for each character. The use of aggregate structures helps to overcome these problems. An aggregate structure is simply a series of scalar variables strung together under (usually) one name. The two of the most common aggregate structures are the record and the array. We will cover them both in detail in this chapter.

Arrays

In general, an array is a collection of variables of the same type. All of the variables in an array are stored sequentially, that is, each variable in the collection directly follows the one before it. Under normal circumstances, when an array is defined, its length is fixed, and cannot be modified. Some modern programming languages do provide tools to dynamically resize an array once it is defined. However, when an array is resized it is usually necessary for the program to move the array to a different location in memory (a very slow process). When an array is defined, it is assigned a single name. To access individual elements of the array a subscript, or index, is used to identify the individual element. In a multidimensional array multiple subscripts are used (2 for a 2 dimensional array, 3 for a 3 dimensional array, etc.)

Array storage

A computer program usually needs more information about your array other than the data that it stores. The computer needs to know the memory address of the first element in your array (the arrays base), the number of elements, and the number of dimensions that your array is defined as having. Depending on how your particular compiler handles arrays, it may store more information about the array such as maximum and minimum values of each element.

The address of each individual element, however, does not necessarily have to be stored. If you have an array of 4 byte integers and you want to access the third element, the computer simply calculates the location of the third element by adding 4*(3-1) to the base address. The location of each element can be calculated this way because the elements of the array are stored consecutively.

A breakdown of calculating an individual array element's position is as follows:

Let BA equal the base address of the array
Let ES equal the size, in bytes, of each element
Let I equal the index of the element to be located

The element's address = BA + (ES * I)

Therefore, if you wanted to view element 5 of an array of 1-byte characters stored at location 242 the resulting address would be:

242 + (1 * 5) = 247

One-dimensional arrays

One-dimensional arrays are the simplest type of array. One-dimensional arrays are used for many applications, including the storage of character strings (such as the phrase "Hello, World!"). They are also useful for storing data that needs to be precalculated (or is useful to precalculate) before use such as a table of sines or cosines.

To address an individual array element, many programming languages enclose the index inside a set of square brackets or in a set of parentheses. Depending on your choice of programming languages this may be different, but the concept should be the same. For example to address element 5 in an array named myarray I would type "myarray[5]" to indicate that I wanted to access the sixth element of the array myarray.

Array elements are usually indexed starting at 0. Therefore, the elements in a 5-element array would be numbered sequentially from 0-4 (the fifth element in an array of 5 elements is addressed as element 4, just as the first element is addressed as element 0).

Multi-dimensional arrays

Multidimensional arrays are a natural extension of one-dimensional arrays. Multi-dimensional arrays can be used to simplify many cases where using many one-dimensional arrays would be tedious. For example, a simple spreadsheet program would use an array of 2 dimensions to store its cell data. Using a series of one-dimensional arrays would be difficult to implement in such a case.

Visualization of a multi-dimensional array is important as it allows you to "see" the structure of your data, as you desire to view it. You can visualize multi-dimensional arrays in different ways:

You can view a two-dimensional array as a table with rows and columns.

You can view a three-dimensional array as a group of two-dimensional arrays forming a cube.

You can view four-dimensional array as a group of cubes.

For higher dimensional arrays, it is best to draw on paper how you want to visualize the data. This sketch will help eliminate confusion when you are writing your program. Some people even recommend sketching your multi-dimensional array structure for any multi-dimensional array that you use in your program. When you first start using multi-dimensional arrays in your programs, this type of support can be invaluable.

Addressing the individual elements of an array can be confusing. Individual elements in a multi-dimensional array are indexed using a separate subscript for each dimension. The size of each dimension is defined when the array is declared and when addressing elements each dimension is ordered in the order defined in the declaration. For example, a two-dimensional array would use two subscripts to identify a single element. Using our row/column analogy to access an element at the visual bottom right corner of array R declared as an integer array with five rows and six columns we would type "R [4,5]". (We use 4,5 instead of 5,6 because the elements are numbered starting at 0, so the element at index 4 would be the fifth element in the row and the element at index 5 would be the sixth element in the column). For higher dimensional arrays, this indexing system can get confusing, which is why visualization of a multi-dimensional array is important.

Storage of Multi-Dimensional Arrays

Because memory is addressed in a linear fashion (much like a one-dimensional array), representing a multi-dimensional array in memory can be difficult, especially for arrays with more than three dimensions. For our purposes, we will show how a simple two-dimensional array can be stored in memory.

A character array R of two dimensions is defined with (using the row/column analogy) two rows and five columns. The visual representation would be:

	0	1	2	3	4
0	H	E	L	L	O
1	W	O	R	L	D

If the array were stored in memory in row/column form, the array would look like:

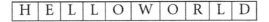

If the array were stored in column/row form, the array would look like:

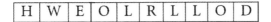

It is more typical to store the array in the order that the dimensions are defined. So if we had a 3 dimensional array, with the dimensions 2x5x2, where each "table" contained the same data the earlier array would be stored like:

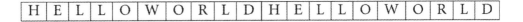

Understanding how a multi-dimensional array is stored in memory is important when trying to determine the memory address of an element in an array. Different compilers can store multi-dimensional arrays differently. In order to calculate the position of an array element you must know the arrays dimensions, how the array is stored in memory, the size of each element, and the memory address of the first element of the array.

Strings of Characters

Many modern programming languages allow you to define an array of characters using a special type. This type is typically called a string. A string is a simple one-dimensional array of character types. You cannot typically address a specific element of a string, as a string isn't defined as an array of characters in languages that support the string type. String types are typically dynamic arrays that are resized as necessary to make it convenient to use strings of characters in your programs. Strings are typically managed using a set of functions that relate to string manipulation that are unique to each implementation. You should consult your language's documentation to see if it supports the string type and what functions are associated with the use of that type.

In programming languages that do not support the string type, you can usually emulate it by using an array of characters and the functions available for dynamically changing the size of an array. Usually, changing the size of the array involves creating a new array of the new size, coping the data from the original array into the new array, deleting the old array, and pointing the old array's variable to the new array. However, you can sometimes find functions that perform this process for you.

Records

You could use arrays in an associative way to store information that relates to other information but must be of different types. For example, you could have two arrays, one that holds an account number (integer) and one that holds an account balance (float). You could relate the data by saying that the account number in the first array at index N relates to the account with a balance in the second array at location N. However, if you were storing large amounts of data this way, you could easily make a mistake when writing your program which could lead to a logical error that would be very difficult to locate. (A logical error is one that the computer cannot detect, like calculating a persons age to be 1,024. The code could be correct as far as the computer is concerned, but the program doesn't function as expected.) Records allow one to manage related information in a simple and structured way.

A record is similar to a one-dimensional array except that a record can contain elements of different types. If you've ever worked with a database system you've seen the use of records as rows in a table. Some languages, such as the C programming language, call the record type by a different name. Some languages call the record type a "structure" and some call the record type a "type". Whatever the name, record type allows similar functionality.

When creating a record, one first creates the records definition. The definition includes the name of the record's structure and the types (in the order you desire them) that make up the record. Once a record is defined you can create a variable, or array, of the type of your record's structure. Here is a pseudocode example to show how records are created and elements are accessed.

create a record called MyRec with an Integer named A and a Float named B
create a variable called NewRec of type MyRec
set NewRec.A = 10
set NewRec.B = 10.5

You can see from the example that creating a record's definition, in effect, creates a new aggregate variable type. The dot operator shown in the above example is one of the most common ways to access a record's elements. A record element can be of any type (even an array or another record) and you can create an array of records of your record type. Record elements are typically called fields.

Records are stored in memory the same way that an array would be stored, with one element following the other. An array of records would be stored the same way that a two dimensional array would be stored. Arrays of records, especially arrays of records that contain arrays, can grow large in size very quickly. You should be careful to limit the size of arrays used in records, and the size of the arrays of records, to avoid using too much memory.

Chapter 3 Exercises

Answer the following questions as being true or false:

1) The memory address of each element in an array must be known.
2) An array is a collection of variables of the same type.
3) The base address of an array is the location of the first element.
4) The index of the third element in an array with 5 elements is 3.
5) You can visualize a 2 dimensional array as a cube.

Answer the following questions to the best of your ability:

6) What would the memory address of the array element indexed as 3 be if the base address of the array of characters is 1020?
7) Can a record contain fields of any scalar or aggregate type?
8) How many subscripts does it take to reference an element in a 3 dimensional array?
9) What is the index of the first element in a one-dimensional array?
10) Define an aggregate structure
11) Can a string be considered a 2 dimensional array?
12) Which of the following would be best suited to store large amounts of related data of different types?

    A) Associated arrays
    B) An array of records
    C) A 2 dimensional array
    D) Any aggregate structure

13) Which of the following would be best suited to store large amounts of related data of the same type?

    A) Associated arrays
    B) An array of records
    C) A 2 dimensional array
    D) Any aggregate structure

14) A string would be an example of what aggregate structure?

15) What steps are involved (typically) when creating a record?

4

Basic Sorting Algorithms

One of the most common operations performed on arrays is a sort. A sort is an operation that orders a list of data in an array in a certain way. If you were to sort a list of numbers in ascending order, the smallest number would appear first in the array and the largest number would appear last. If you were storing a list of peoples names and addresses, you would want the data sorted by name before you printed the list. Sorting algorithms are methods that allow you to order your data.

There are many different ways that a program can sort data. Some sorting algorithms are faster than others while some are simpler to implement. When you decide to use a sorting algorithm in your program, you must also decide what algorithm is best to use. So far, no one has discovered a sorting algorithm that acts as a "catch all" that is always the best solution to the problem. For that reason, we will cover two very common sorting techniques that can be used in many situations where sorting is needed.

Bubble Sort

The first sort we will discuss is commonly called a bubble sort. You may sometimes hear this type of sort referred to as an exchange sort. The bubble sort is called a bubble sort because in practice it appears that the items that belong in the upper most portion float like bubbles in a liquid to the upper most portion.

A bubble sort works by making several passes through the array to be sorted, checking adjacent pairs of values to determine whether they are in or out of order. If they are out of order, the numbers in the pair exchange positions, effectively putting that pair in the proper order. By continuously passing through the array until no exchanges are made, the array will be sorted in the order that you desired. You can use a Boolean variable (set to false at the beginning of each pass, and set to true if an exchange was made) to see if any exchanges were made during the latest pass. If no exchanges were made (the Boolean variable is false) then the list is sorted.

Here is an example of a bubble sort in action:

The original Array: 22 33 45 87 12 32
The First Pass:

Compare	Array	Exchange
0 and 1	(22 33) 45 87 12 32	
1 and 2	22 (33 45) 87 12 32	
2 and 3	22 33 (45 87) 12 32	
3 and 4	22 33 45 (87 12) 32	Yes
4 and 5	22 33 45 12 (87 32)	Yes

The Second Pass

Compare	Array	Exchange
0 and 1	(22 33) 45 12 32 87	
1 and 2	22 (33 45) 12 32 87	
2 and 3	22 33 (45 12) 32 87	Yes
3 and 4	22 33 12 (45 32) 87	Yes

Compare	Array	Exchange
4 and 5	22 33 12 32 (45 87)	

The Third Pass

Compare	Array	Exchange
0 and 1	(22 33) 12 32 45 87	
1 and 2	22 (33 12) 32 45 87	Yes
2 and 3	22 12 (33 32) 45 87	Yes
3 and 4	22 12 32 (33 45) 87	
4 and 5	22 12 32 33 (45 87)	

The Fourth Pass

Compare	Array	Exchange
0 and 1	(22 12) 32 33 45 87	Yes
1 and 2	12 (22 32) 33 45 87	
2 and 3	12 22 (32 33) 45 87	
3 and 4	12 22 32 (33 45) 87	
4 and 5	12 22 32 33 (45 87)	

The Fifth Pass

Compare	Array	Exchange
0 and 1	(22 12) 32 33 45 87	
1 and 2	12 (22 32) 33 45 87	
2 and 3	12 22 (32 33) 45 87	

Compare	Array	Exchange
3 and 4	12 22 32 (33 45) 87	
4 and 5	12 22 32 33 (45 87)	

No exchanges were made in the last pass so the list must be sorted.

Optimizing the bubble sort

An analysis of the algorithm will show that with each successive pass at least one array element is placed in its final position at the bottom portion of the array. This effectively divides the array into a sorted and unsorted section. By taking advantage of this feature we can calculate the maximum number of passes required to sort the array. We can also reduce the number of comparisons in a pass by one for each iteration.

The first pass requires that each pair be compared. The second pass requires one less comparison because we know that the last digit in the array is in its proper position. The third pass requires one less comparison than the second as the next to the last digit is in its proper place. By limiting the number of comparisons we can sort the array much faster.

This feature also allows us to calculate the maximum number of passes through the array by simply subtracting 1 from the total number of elements in the array. So an array with 10 elements would require a maximum of 9 passes through the array.

Lets assume that the number of passes performed is stored in an integer called NP. NP would be equal to 0 at the start of the search and increment by one after each pass. We will also create an integer variable called NC which will store the number of comparisons necessary. NC will be recalculated at each pass to be equal to one less than the total number of elements in the array minus the value of NP. Comparisons will be made until the value of NC is reached in each pass. If NC is equal to 0 when it is recalculated then the sort is complete. The sort will also be complete if the Boolean variable we created in the original program is set to false. Please note that the adjustments to the algorithm I explained here are for clarity purposes only and a different method to implement the optimization can be used when actually implementing the sort. Here is a pseudocode example of the optimized bubble sort algorithm.

1 create an array of integer types called MyArray of length 5
2 Fill the array MyArray with random numbers
3 create an integer variable called NP and set its value equal to 0
4 create an integer variable called AL and set its value to 5
5 create a Boolean variable called Exchanged and set its value to False
6 create an integer variable called P and set its value to 0
7 create an integer variable called Temp and set its value to 0
8 create an integer variable called NC and set its value to 0
9 check to see if NP is equal to AL - 1 if so then goto step 19
10 set Exchanged equal to False
11 set NC = (AL–1)–NP
12 check to see if P is equal to NC if so then goto step 16
13 check to see if MyArray [P] is greater than MyArray [P+1]

   if so do the following:
   13A set Exchanged equal to True
   13B set Temp equal to MyArray [P]
   13C set MyArray [P] equal to Myarray [P+1]
   13D set MyArray [P+1] equal to Temp

14 set P equal to P+1
15 goto step 10
16 set NP equal to NP+1
17 check to see if Exchanged is equal to False if so then goto step 19
18 goto step 10
19 end the program

The Selection Sort

The next sort we will discuss is known as the selection sort. For our purposes we will use the simple straight selection or "jump down" sort. The selection sort makes fewer exchanges than the bubble sort, however, unlike the bubble sort (where we can immediately stop the search when no exchanges have been made, saving processing time in an already or almost sorted list) the selection sort requires that a fixed number of passes be made.

The selection sort works by searching through the array until the next item desired is found and places it in its position (performing a swap). It always makes N-1 passes through the array, no matter if the list is sorted or not.

Let's take a look at the selection sort at work:

The original Array: 22 33 45 87 12 32
last value = 0 (Lval)
last position = 0 (Lpos)
current position: 5
The First Pass:

Array	Eval	Lval	Lpos
[22] 33 45 87 12 32	22>0	22	0
22 [33] 45 87 12 32	33>22	33	1
22 33 [45] 87 12 32	45>33	45	2
22 33 45 [87] 12 32	87>45	87	3
22 33 45 87 [12] 32	12<87	87	3
22 33 45 87 12 [32]	33<87	87	3

Swap values at current position and last position
22 33 45 32 12 87

current position: 4
last value = 0
last position = 0

The Second Pass:

Array	Eval	Lval	Lpos
[22] 33 45 32 12 87	22>0	22	0
22 [33] 45 32 12 87	33>22	33	1
22 33 [45] 32 12 87	45>33	45	2
22 33 45 [32] 12 87	32<45	45	2
22 33 45 32 [12] 87	12<45	45	2

Swap values at current position and last position
22 33 12 32 45 87

current position: 3
last value = 0
last position = 0

The Third Pass:

Array	Eval	Lval	Lpos
[22] 33 12 32 45 87	22>0	22	0
22 [33] 12 32 45 87	33>22	33	1
22 33 [12] 32 45 87	12<33	33	1
22 33 12 [32] 45 87	32<33	33	1

Swap values at current position and last position
22 32 12 33 45 87

current position: 2
last value = 0
last position = 0

The Fourth Pass:

Array	Eval	Lval	Lpos
[22] 32 12 33 45 87	22>0	22	0
22 [32] 12 33 45 87	32>22	32	1
22 32 [12] 33 45 87	12<32	32	1

Swap values at current position and last position
22 12 32 33 45 87
current position: 2
last value = 0
last position = 0

The Fifth Pass:

Array	Eval	Lval	Lpos
[22] 12 32 33 45 87	22>0	22	0
22 [12] 32 33 45 87	12<22	22	0

Swap values at current position and last position
12 22 32 33 45 87—The List is sorted

In the above example I keep track of the current position whose value I'm looking for, the largest number I've found so far, and the aforementioned numbers index. With each pass through the array I make one less comparison. If I didn't make one less comparison in each pass then the array would never get sorted, as it would just move the largest value in the array from the last element to the second element.

Here is some pseudocode for implementing a selection sort:

1 create an integer array named MyArray with a length of 5
2 fill the MyArray array with random numbers
3 create an integer variable named LP and set its value equal to 0
4 create an integer variable named LV and set its value equal to 0
5 create an integer variable named CP and set its value equal to 4

6 create an integer variable named P and set its value equal to 0

7 create an integer variable named Temp and set its value equal to 0

8 check to see if CP is equal to 0 if so then goto step 21

9 set LP equal to 0

10 set LV equal to 0

11 set P equal to 0

12 check to see if P is equal to CP if so then goto step 16

13 check to see if MyArray [P] > LV if so then do the following:

    13A set LV equal to MyArray [P]

    13B set LP equal to P

14 set P equal to P+1

15 goto step 12

16 set Temp equal MyArray [LP]

17 set MyArray [LP] equal to MyArray [CP]

18 set MyArray [CP] equal to Temp

19 set CP equal to CP − 1

20 goto step 8

21 end program

Notes on the stability of sorting algorithms

Let's assume for an example that we have an array of records that stores a list of names and a list of zip codes that we wanted to sort alphabetically and grouped by zip code. We would first have to sort the list by name (the field "name" would be the sorts key) to list them all alphabetically. Then we would sort the list of names by zip code (the field "zipcode" would be the sorts key in this case) so that we would have a list of names listed alphabetically by groups of zip codes. The algorithm sounds simple enough, but when we run our program, the list is sorted by zip code, but the names are not listed alphabetically under each group. What could have caused the problem?

The problem arose when we sorted the list by zip code, naturally. When we wrote the program we used a selection sort to sort the names alphabetically and a selection sort to sort the names by zip code. The problem lies in the sorting algorithm. A selection sort is an unstable sort. An unstable sorting algorithm doesn't preserve the order of the previous sort.

A stable sorting algorithm would solve this problem. A stable sort preserves the existing order of the first key while it orders the rest of the data. When we perform a sort in the fashion listed above it doesn't matter what sorting algorithm we use for the first sort, as we are not concerned with preserving the lists order, but the second (and possibly third or fourth) sort must be performed with a stable sort.

So in order to solve our problem, we replace the second sort with a bubble sort. A bubble sort is an easy to implement stable sorting algorithm that solves our problem nicely. It is important to keep the stability or instability of a sort in mind when choosing what type of sorting algorithm to use in your programs. Strange errors like the one listed above happen all the time and can be incredibly difficult to detect.

Chapter 4 Exercises

1) What does a sort do?

2) A bubble sort is sometimes referred to as what?

3) Describe the action of a bubble sort.

4) What advantages does a bubble sort have over a selection sort.

5) What makes a sorting algorithm stable?

6) Does the stability of a sorting algorithm matter when sorting a one-dimensional array and why?

7) Describe the action of a selection sort.

8) How does one calculate the maximum number of passes that a bubble sort will take before completion?

9) How does one calculate the number of passes that a selection sort will make before completion?

10) Under what conditions will a bubble sort terminate?

5

Basic Searching Algorithms

You will find that when writing different software applications, that it is necessary to locate a certain piece of information in a data structure. For example, lets assume that you had an array of records with the fields account number, name, and account balance and you wanted to find out how much a person with a certain account number has in his or her account. In order to find that piece of information you, would have to perform a search on your array to determine in what array index that that person's account information resides.

In order to perform a search on any data structure, you must determine a way to transverse that data structure so that every element in the structure can be accessed. With the simple data structures we have been working with, the transversal isn't a problem so we can focus on specific searching techniques.

I'd like to introduce some terminology at this point to help simplify the rest of this chapter.

Key

One of the most important elements of a search is called the key. The key is the field on which you perform the search. For example, if I were to perform the search from my earlier example the account number field would be my search key. The key is usually left unchanged after the search is performed as your usually looking to either find information or change information that is associated with a particular key. For example, to update a persons phone number or account balance based on their account number.

Criteria

Another important aspect of a search is called the criteria. The "criteria" is what you are searching for. If I were to search a list of client information looking for the name of the person whose account number is "31337" then the number "31337" would be my search criteria. I would perform my search for that account number by comparing my criteria to the value of each element in the list of keys (the account number field in this case).

Linear Search

The simplest type of search that you can perform is the linear, or sequential, search. This type of search is easy to implement, and can be used in just about any case where you must perform a search on a data structure. The linear search works by examining each individual key in your list until it finds one that matches your criteria. This type of search is useful for searching an unsorted list for a particular key. Searching a sorted list using the linear search method is less efficient than using other search methods.

In the absolute worst-case scenario, a linear search will examine every key without finding a match. If your search through a large amount of data, this could take some time. It is best to use a linear search only when a nominal amount of data is being examined and not as a standard search to be implemented exclusively in your program.

When you perform a linear search on a set of keys, only the first key that matches your criteria will be returned. You can modify a linear search algorithm to return every matching key, however, in doing so your algorithm will be forced to check your criteria against every key in your data set.

Here is a pseudocode listing of a linear search algorithm:

(For this example we are assuming that you have an array of records (a record set) named INFO with 100 elements containing the an integer field named AN that holds account numbers, and a float field named AB that holds account balances that is already filled with data)

1 create a variable of type integer named CI and set its value to 0
2 create a variable of type integer named CRITERIA and set its value to 31337
3 create a variable of type integer named LOC and set its value to –1
4 check to see if CI is equal to 100 if so goto step 9
5 check to see if INFO[CI].AN is equal to CRITERIA if so do the following:

    5A set LOC equal to CI

6 check to see if LOC is greater than -1 if so then goto step 9
7 set CI equal to CI+1
8 goto step 4
9 check to see if LOC is greater than -1 if so then do the following:

    9A display INFO[LOC].AB on the screen

10 check to see if LOC is equal to -1 if so then do the following:

    10A display "Account Number Not Found" on the screen

11 end program

Our example program searches the record set until it finds the index that holds the key that matches our criteria. If none of the keys match our criteria, then the value of LOC is equal to -1. If a key matches our criteria then the value of LOC is equal to the index of the record that matches our criteria. You can see how simple a linear search is to implement in a program.

Binary Search

The binary search is a more advanced algorithm useful for searching a list of information that is already sorted. A binary search will not work in an unsorted array. Also, a binary search must search using the key that was most recently sorted.

A binary search is performed by the computer in the same way that a regular person would search for an entry in a dictionary. You start by opening the dictionary to the middle, then you look to either the left portion of the dictionary or the right portion and continue to divide the book into sections until you have found the page that contains the entry that you desire.

Being a human, if you know that the word you desire to be defined begins with the letter A then you can begin looking more towards the front of the dictionary instead of the exact middle. A computer, on the other hand, doesn't have such an advantage. The computer must begin looking in the exact center of the book and make a decision as towards which half contains the information desired. When it picks a half it continues looking in the exact center of the chosen half and again makes a decision and divides the resulting section again. This cycle continues until the desired entry is located.

Here is an example of a binary search in action:

We will be searching for the number 26 in the following array:

2 4 6 8 10 12 14 16 18 20 22 24 26 28 30

1) Checking the entry in the middle of the array we determine whether or not the entry we are looking for is to the left (less than) or to the right (greater than) of the current entry.
2 4 6 8 10 12 14 [16] 18 20 22 24 26 28 30
26 is greater than 16

2) Ignoring the leftmost half of our array we compare the middle of the remaining entries to determine what direction to move.
(2 4 6 8 10 12 14 16) 18 20 22 [24] 26 28 30
26 is greater than 24

3) Ignoring the leftmost half of the remaining array segment we compare the middle of the remaining entries to determine what direction to move.
(2 4 6 8 10 12 14 16 18 20 22 24) 26 [28] 30
26 is less than 28

4) Ignoring the rightmost half of the remaining array segment we compare the middle of the remaining entries to determine what direction to move.
(2 4 6 8 10 12 14 16 18 20 22 24) [26] (30)
26 is equal to 26

5) Because the entry we desired has been located, we can record our current position in the whole array to be used as an index to locate related data.

You can see how much faster a binary search algorithm can be when compared to a linear search algorithm. A binary search is incredibly fast because with each comparison we eliminate half of the possible matches in the array. In fact, we can calculate the maximum number of comparisons required to find (or not find) the entry that we desire in the array. All we need to do is calculate how many times a number equal to the number of array elements can be divided by 2 and still remain an integer. A simple formula would be: Log2(N). That is the base 2 logarithm of N where N is the number of elements in our array. Because we have to do more than one comparison to determine whether or not to move in a direction or claim the desired key has been located we need to multiply this result by the number of comparisons made. As little as 2 comparisons are needed to perform these calculations, but three comparisons are useful for example purposes. So our resulting formula would be 2*Log2(N) or 3*Log2(N)

Here is a pseudocode listing of a binary search algorithm:

(For this example, we will assume that we have an array of records (a record set) named INFO of length 100 with an integer field named AN that holds account numbers and a field named AB that holds the account balance related to the account number. We will also assume that the record set is completely populated with information and that the record set is sorted in ascending order)

1 create a variable of type integer named F and set its value to 0

2 create a variable of type integer named M and set its value to 0

3 create a variable of type integer named L and set its value to 99

4 create a variable of type integer named P and set its value to -1

5 create a variable of type integer named C and set its value to 31337

5 check to see if F is equal to L if so then do the following:

> 5A set P equal to F
> 5B check to see if INFO[M].AN is equal to C if so goto step 11
> 5C set P equal to –1
> 5D goto step 12

6 set M equal to (F + L) / 2
7 check to see if INFO[M].AN is equal to C if so the do the following:

> 7A set P equal to M
> 7B goto step 11

8 check to see if INFO[M].AN is less than C if so set F equal to M +1
9 check to see if INFO[M].AN is greater than C if so set L equal to M-1
10 goto step 5
11 check to see if P is greater than -1 if so then do the following:
11A display INFO[P].AN on the screen
12 check to see if P is equal to -1 if so then do the following:
12A display "Account Not Found" on the screen
13 end program

The variables F and L represent the first and last entry in the portion of the record set that we have not yet eliminated. The variable M represents the middle of that group and is calculated in step 6. Remember that when working with integer data, when we divide we will get an integer result. This means that if F is 2 and L is 3 then the result of our division in step 6 will be 2 and not 2.5.

Hashing and Hash Functions

The fastest way to locate an entry in an array, or in a record set, is to not search at all. You could locate an entry much faster than any search by simply calculating the entry's position by performing some arithmetic operation on your search criteria.

A hash function locates data in this way:

A hash function H is used to compute the location of a given key K. Lets assume (for simplicity) that the hash function divides the key by 100 and returns the remainder as the index. If you wanted to find the location of some record related to a key with a value of 638 you would pass 638 as K to the hash function H so H(K) = 38. 38 in this case would be the computed index for the key 638. We would then be able to immediately locate data stored in our record set by using the computed index as our subscript.

When we are adding a new record to our record set, we must first compute its index using our hash function to identify the location that the data belongs in the record set so that we can use the hash function to locate that entry in the record set later.

There are several downsides to using hash functions to locate data. First of all, all your data must be inserted into its proper place in your record set by first computing its desired location using your hash function. It would be difficult, if not impossible, to create a hash function that correctly locates data in a pre-existing record set. (We will use the term hash table to refer to a record set that is populated and searched using a hash function)

Second, a hash function will only work with one key. So, if you build a hash function to locate data in your hash table by, for example, an account number, then you can only search for data using your hash function by the account number.

Finally, creating a hash function that always computes a unique index for each key is notoriously difficult. A hash function that computes a different value (hash number) for each given key is called a perfect hash function. You will sometimes hear a perfect hash function referred to as bijective, meaning that the function produces a unique hash number for each key. A perfect hash function is rarely if ever obtained in practice. When a hash function computes the same hash number for two different key values then a hash collision (or hash crash) occurs and steps must be in place to deal with such a collision.

Hash functions are difficult to design. We will cover a few common types of functions to give you an idea of how hash functions are designed.

On of the simplest types of hash functions to implement, and to design, is a simple division operation. This is one of the first types of hash functions used and is commonly found in smaller programs. This type of hash function assumes that you know the maximum size that you desire your array to be.

An example would be a function that takes a value, X, and divides that number by the maximum size of your array, N, and returns the remainder. Therefore, we could define a hash function F as:

$$F(X) = X \bmod N$$

This type of hash function is prone to collisions (hash clashes). To reduce the number of collisions, you can round the value of N up to the nearest prime number. That is a prime number larger than the size of your array or record set. It has been suggested that a prime number in the form of $4N + 3$ (for an integer N) is particularly good. Although this will not eliminate collisions completely, it should help to reduce them.

Another method that is commonly used is called the midsquare method. This method uses a technique similar to a pseudorandom number generator in an attempt to reduce the number of collisions. The midsquare method is actually a modification of another older technique that uses a pseudorandom number generator exclusively. The idea is that by introducing a certain amount of randomness to the function, two values that would normally return the same values (causing a collision), would receive different values.

This type of hash function operates by first squaring the input number and then taking a few of the digits from the center of the resulting base 10 number to use as the resulting hash number. Therefore, the resulting hash number is composed of the "middle of the square" of the key number. A simple formula to compute these numbers is also commonly used as a pseudorandom number generator.

$$F(X) = (X^2 / 10^N) \bmod 10^N$$

The variable N is usually a small number such as 2 or 4. Even numbers seem to work best.

You can also calculate hash numbers using a technique called bit compression. You may also hear this technique called digit compression or "folding". There is a distinction between bit and digit compression. In bit compression the technique is applied using the base 2 number system, where digit compression typically refers to the operation being performed using the base 10 number system. Either technique can be referred to as folding.

Folding is a more complicated process than most hash functions as it cannot be done in a single arithmetic expression. The techniques involves first dividing the key into X groups of Y digits (the last group can have fewer than Y digits). Second, the groups are combined together using an arithmetic or Boolean operation such as addition or XOR (exclusive or). Finally, some of the least significant digits are used as the hash number. The digits can be extracted, when performing the operation on base 10 numbers, by taking the remainder of a division operation performed on the resulting number of the first calculation and a power of 10 (like the numbers 100, 1000, 10000, etc., depending on the expected size of the resulting numbers)

Here is an example:

For a given key: 123456789
Divide the key into 4 groups of 3 digits: 123, 456, 789, 0
Sum the groups together: 123+456+789+0 = 1368
Take the last few digits: 1368 mod 1000 = 368

A technique similar to folding is digit analysis. Digit analysis involves simply sampling a few of the digits in the key and then rearranging them in some fashion to form the hash number. This technique isn't as desirable as other techniques because fewer parts of the key are used. This could cause 2 very different numbers to be evaluated in the same way leading to a hash collision. To make better use of this technique, it should be applied to other hash functions to remove bias digits. A bias digit is one that appears more often than other digits in a given key. For example, all credit cards of the same type start with the same four digits. If you were building a hash table that is to be searched by credit card number, then you would want to remove the first four digits before calculating the hash number as these digits are bias. A bias digit could also be a digit that appears more commonly than another. If, for example, a statistical analysis of account numbers that you issue shows that the last digit is usually a 5 or 7 then the last digit is bias and could be removed before performing the hash function.

The final method I will discuss is called the multiplication method. This method give a very good distribution of hash numbers for a given set of keys, but requires two extra functions to be defined in order to be implemented properly. It is known as the multiplication method because of the 2 multiplication operations that are preformed. The formula is as follows:

$$F(X) = truncate(Y * fraction(X * Z))$$

The value Y is the maximum size of your hash table. The truncate function returns the integer part of a floating point number (removes the fractional part of a number) and the fraction function returns the fractional part of a number (removes the integer part of a number). X is the key value that is passed to the hash function (as shown in the definition F (X)). Z in a number between 0 and 1 exclusive (that is greater than 0 and less than 1).

Picking a good value for Z can be difficult. You can use trial and error to determine what value is best to use or you can use a pseudorandom number generator that you seed with the key and reduce to a number greater than 0 and less than 1. Many people, however, say that the number 0.618034 or 0.381966 (the square root of 5 minus 1 divided by 2 and 1 minus the square root of 5 minus 1 divided by 2, respectively) works best for the value of Z in this type of hash function.

Building the functions truncate and fraction can be daunting for a novice programmer. Fortunately, there is a simple method that takes advantage of how many computer languages handle scalar data types. Most modern computer languages allow you to change the type of a variable temporarily when used in an arithmetic operation. You might remember this when we discussed types. We will take advantage of the loss of precision when casting a float type to an integer type.

In order to find the integer part of a floating-point number, for the truncate function, simply cast the value that was passed to the function to an integer and return that value.

To find just the fractional part of a floating-point number, for the fraction function, simply subtract the integer value of the value that was passed to the function from itself. You could even use your truncate function here. If we had a function called T that acted like our truncate function then we could define a function F that acts as the fraction function like: $F(X) = X - T(X)$

If your programming language doesn't support type casting, you can usually find a function that rounds a number. A function that rounds a number typically acts to remove the fractional part of the number without bothering to round up or down. (one usually has to add .5 to a number to make the function round up for numbers whose fractional part are greater than 0.5 and round down for numbers whose fractional parts are less than 0.5) If your programming language has such a function, you can use it to replace the truncate function.

Chapter 5 Exercises

1) What is the purpose of a search function?

2) Define the term "key" and how it is used.

3) Define the term "criteria" and how it is used.

4) What is the most efficient method for searching a presorted list?

5) Describe how a binary search operates.

6) Show how you would calculate the maximum number of comparisons required to find or not find a desired entry in an array of 100 elements when using a binary search.

7) How does a hash function locate data?

8) Describe thee downsides to using hash functions.

9) Describe three types of hash functions.

10) Describe and give an example of a collision.

6

Linked Lists

A linked list is an abstract data type, composed of a collection of records that are used to emulate an array or record set. Each entry in a linked list is called a node. A node is a record that contains at least 2 fields, a data field that contains the information to be stored, and an address field that points to the next node in the list. A node can have any number of data fields of any legal type. A node many also have more than one address field. A node with more than one address field typically has 2 address fields; one pointing to the next node in the list (commonly named the next field), and one pointing back to the previous node in the list. A linked list composed of a group of nodes that utilizes 2 address fields is called a doubly linked list. A linked list composed of a group of nodes that utilizes a single address field is called a singly linked list.

An address field is commonly called a pointer. A pointer is a variable, usually the size of a long integer, that stores a memory address and is used to reference another variable. (Remember that every variable is represented at some location in memory). The language under which you choose to implement a linked list must support some form of pointer type. (Note: There are methods to imitate linked lists in languages like Java™ where there are no visible pointers. However, the methods are exceptionally complicated and don't offer the

THE BOOK ON DATA STRUCTURES

flexibility, usability, and speed that the pointer method does. You can usually find an alternative to a linked list when pointers are not available.)

It is important to keep in mind that a pointer doesn't represent the actual location of the node that it points to. A pointer simply represents the memory address of the node. When you're writing code this distinction can become unclear or confusing. You must be clear on the distinction between the pointer and the object it points to in order to properly use linked lists. Let's pretend that a node in your list is named Bob. Bob is standing in a room full of people. Let's also pretend that across the room is a pointer named Poindexter that is directing people towards Bob by pointing at him. Poindexter would be the next field in the node above Bob. Bob would be the node that Poindexter is directing people toward. Notice that Bob and Poindexter are in different locations. The address of the pointer is different than the address of the node it is pointing to. However, the value of the pointer is the same as the address of the node it points to.

The first node in a linked list is called the head of the list, or the head node. The last node in the list is called the tail, or tail node. The next field of the tail node usually contains a null pointer. A null pointer is a pointer that usually points to memory address 0 and is used to indicate the end of the list. The null pointer is typically represented by a language's implementation of null, a zero value, or a forward slash (/). A null pointer is sometimes called a "dummy" address.

The data items in a linked list can be retrieved in an order that doesn't necessarily reflect their physical memory locations. Here is an example:

Take a linked list shown with the memory address, data field, and next field. Note that the memory address are shown in base 16

0001	A	0006
0006	D	000B
000B	E	null

Right now the order of the data items is a direct reflection of their respective memory locations. But what happens when we add 2 items to the list called B and C and insert them into the linked list in their respective alphabetic position.

0001	A	0010
0006	D	000B
000B	E	null
0010	B	0015
0015	C	0006

You can see that node A points to B, and B to C, and so on. Right now the order of the nodes does not reflect their respective positions in memory.

Representing linked lists

You have already seen how a linked list can be represented in memory from the previous example. I'd like to discuss common ways that linked lists are represented for design and debugging purposes.

You will often see linked lists represented as rectangular boxes (subdivided into fields) representing nodes. Arrows are drawn between nodes to show the values of the pointers (what node the pointers are assigned to). An example of such a representation (in an order that reflects its order in memory) would be:

The nodes can be labeled by their respective order in the list, the order of their creation, or their order in memory, really in any ordered sequence. The arrows (representing links) can be labeled as well, but it isn't necessary. Also, The addresses listed in the "next" field need not be listed as the arrows represent the pointers address accurately enough.

You have already sent he other way to represent a linked list earlier in this chapter. That is, a representation of the linked list in memory. This is usually formatted in the same way that I formatted it above. There are, however, two ways that you may see this type of representation shown. The first is to represent the memory addresses as real addresses in the segment: offset format

(0000:0001) or just the offset (0001). The second way is to represent the memory addresses as simple integers, as if the starting address of each record were numbered sequentially, usually starting at 1 (although it is more appropriate to start at 0, starting at 1 seems common for this purpose). I will show examples of each.

(For the following examples, we will assume that each record contains two fields, a data field composes of a single character type and a "next" field that contains a pointer to the next node in the list.)

The first method
Segment: offset format

0000:0001	A	0000:0010
0000:0006	D	0000:000B
0000:000B	E	null
0000:0010	B	0000:0015
0000:0015	C	0000:0006

Offset format

0001	A	0010
0006	D	000B
000B	E	null
0010	B	0015
0015	C	0006

The second method

1	A	4
2	D	3
3	E	null

4	B	5
5	C	2

The best way to represent a linked list is an exact imitation of how its data is stored in memory. This method is useful for debugging errors that deal with memory allocation and deallocation. Each field is represented beside its individual memory address in segment: offset style. The addresses are shown in base 16. The field's data should be shown in a manner most accurate for representing itself (i.e. a pointer would be in base 16 in segment: offset format, but an integer would be in base 10). Here is an example:

0000:0001	A
0000:0002	0000:0010
0000:0006	D
0000:0007	0000:000B
0000:000B	E
0000:000C	0000:0000
0000:0010	B
0000:0011	0000:0015
0000:0015	C
0000:0016	0000:0006

No matter how you choose to diagram a linked list, the information about the lists structure remains the same. Each diagram has its advantages or disadvantages depending on its use, but the decision to use a particular diagram is always your choice to make.

In the examples above, you can see some of the advantages of using linked lists over arrays. The most obvious advantage is the fact that nodes in the list are added dynamically. That is, you don't preallocate a large list of nodes during the coding phase, but instead add nodes as they are needed at runtime. This allows your to use memory more efficiently as you only use memory as it is needed. Remember, if you have an array of characters of length 100, you are using 100 bytes of memory even if there is no data stored in that array. A linked list doesn't have such a disadvantage.

Another advantage comes when inserting data into the array. If you wanted to add an entry to the middle of an array, you would have to shift every entry in the array below the insertion point down. If you insert your entry near the top of a large array, that move could take a significant amount of time to complete. With a linked list, however, an insertion only requires that maximum of 2 pointers be changed. This process takes much less time to complete than moving even 2 entries in an array down one position. Deleting items from a linked list is equally advantageous to deleting an item from an array as a maximum of 2 pointers need to be updated to complete the operation. Deleting an item in an array could mean shifting as many as all of the remaining items in the array up one position.

There are many disadvantages to the use of linked lists over arrays as well. Because the items in a linked list must be accessed in a sequential manner, in order to locate a specific data item, the list must be transversed to the point that the desired item is listed. For example, to find the 17th node in a linked list, one must start at the top of the list, and read the location of each successive node until the 17th node is reached. In contrast, to access the 17th item in an array one simply references the entry directly.

Another disadvantage concerns memory usage. For each node in the list, an extra amount of memory is needed (usually 4 bytes) to be used as a pointer to the next item in the list. For example, assuming that a pointer is four bytes, if we had a linked list with 100 nodes and an array or length 100 storing the same type of data, the linked list would be 400 bytes larger than the array due to the extra space necessary to store the location of the next item in the list.

Up to this point, we have only discussed an implicit implementation of linked lists. Implicitly implementing a linked list is the most common, and most practical, way to implement a linked list. There are, however, 2 ways of implementing a linked list Implicitly (as we have been doing) and explicitly. Explicit implementation of a linked list is uncommon and can be difficult to implement. However, when pointer type variables are not available explicitly implementing a linked list is the only way to utilize this abstract data type.

Explicit implementation

The most common way to explicitly implement a linked list is to use a linear implementation. A linear implementation uses an array of records to mimic actual memory space to overcome the lack of pointers in a particular language. This type of implementation is reminiscent of an earlier example in this chapter where we abstracted the memory addresses in a diagram of a linked list to simple numbers.

When we use a linear implementation, we loose the advantage of using less memory initially in our program. This is because when we create our array, we make it larger than the maximum number of nodes that we intend to program to use. We do this to avoid any loss of performance due to the resizing of an array at run-time. You can choose to resize the array every time a node is inserted or deleted, but it isn't recommended as your program would suffer an incredible loss in performance.

To simplify this section, we will go through the steps necessary to create a linked list of this type. This will give you a better understanding of this type of implementation, as well as an outline to use when creating a linked list in this manner.

The first step in creating a linked list of this type is to create a record type named NODETYPE to define how our nodes are structured. Our type will have 2 fields, a field called DATA of type character and a field called NEXT of type integer. The data field will store a single letter (we will create a linked list to store the letters of the alphabet for this example). The NEXT field will be used to store the index of the next node in the list. In essence, the data in the NEXT field will be used emulate a pointer by using the properties of an array to emulate actual memory.

The next step is to create an array of NODETYPE types. We will name the array NODE, for simplicity, and will define its length to be 27 because that is the maximum number of nodes that we intend to store. (The first node in the array is not used.) This array will be used to store active and inactive nodes. An active node is a node that is considered to be part of our linked list. An inactive node is not considered part of our linked list and can only become active if a node is inserted into our linked list. When the program is running, our array will be an intermingled list of active and inactive nodes. We need to define active and inactive nodes because the memory for all our nodes is allocated whether we use a particular node or not. In an implicitly defined linked list, inactive nodes do not exist as the memory for an individual node is allocated or deallocated when a node is created or destroyed.

The next step is to initialize our array. Initialization links all of our nodes together in a sequential order. Because all of our nodes are currently part of the inactive node set, we can quickly link them together by assigning each node (starting at NODE[1]) equal to the index of the next node in the array so that NODE[1].NEXT = 2, NODE[2].NEXT = 3, etc. We could define this as NODE[N].NEXT = N+1. The last node in the array (NODE[26]) will be zero (our equivalent of null as the first node isn't used). We will create a variable named INACT of type integer that holds the index of the next available node. We will set the value of INACT to be equal to 1 to show that NODE[1] is the next available node in the inactive portion of our array.

When adding, or removing, nodes from the active portion of our array, certain steps have to be taken to ensure that the inactive portion of our array stays sane. That is, we do not accidentally "lose" a node that would other wise be available. When a node is inserted into to the linked list, its position in our array is determined by the current value in the INACT variable. The INACT variable is then reassigned to be the value that NODE[INACT].NEXT was before the insertion took place. When a node is removed from the list, the NEXT field at the position of the removed node is set to the current value of INACT, and the value of INACT is assigned to be equal to the index of the node that was removed. This way, all the inactive nodes remain linked together no matter what order nodes are added and removed.

It is important to ensure that when inserting a node into the list that we have an inactive node to use. An easy way is to check to see if the value of INACT is equal to 0. If INACT is equal to 0 during an insertion operation we can be assured that all of the available (inactive) nodes have been used to store active nodes (nodes that are members of our linked list). If INACT is equal to 0, your insertion function should fail and return an error. If you don't flag this error then other, unpredictable logic errors could appear in your program that would be difficult to trace back to your insertion function.

It is important to note that when inserting a node at the end of the active portion of the array (the last item in the linked list) that the NEXT field be set to null (0 in our case). If the NEXT field is not changed then it is likely that when transversing the linked list, you will run into the inactive portion of the list. This can cause problems, as you shouldn't be able to "see" the inactive items when interfacing with the linked list because the inactive items are not considered part of the linked list.

When inserting nodes into the middle of the linked list, it is important to follow the procedures outlined earlier in this chapter. That is, the node that sits above the node you are inserting should point to the new node, and the new node should point to the item that the node above the inserted node was pointing to. Failing to follow this procedure could easily break your list, causing logic errors, and perhaps even real runtime errors in your program.

The next step involves the creation of our insertion and deletion functions to add and remove nodes from our list. The first function we will describe will be the insertion function.

Create a function called INSERTNODE that takes an integer named POS that is the actual array index of the node to insert the new node below as a parameter and returns an integer value. First, the function will check to see if there are any available nodes and terminate with an error if there are none available. The function will then create a variable named TEMP and set its value equal to INACT. The function will then set the value of INACT to be equal to the value of NODE[INACT].NEXT. If the value of POS is greater than zero then the function will assign the value of NODE[INACT].NEXT equal to the value of NODE[POS].NEXT, otherwise it will assign the value of NODE[INACT].NEXT equal to zero. Next, the function will set NODE[POS].NEXT equal to the value of TEMP if and only if the value of POS is greater than zero. The function will then return the value of TEMP.

The function INSERTNODE should be called only in an assignment statement, so that you know the index in the array that the new node was created. If you wanted the returned pointer to be in variable P you could assign the value of P to be equal to INSERTNODE[N] where N is your current position in the array (obtained by transversing the array). You could then assign a value to DATA in the new node you created by assigning the value of NODE[P].DATA equal to any value you desire.

The INSERTNODE function works by accepting a "pointer" to the node that you want your new node inserted below. If you pass zero to the INSERT-NODE function, it will assume that it is adding the first node in the list. You should not try to empty your linked list by passing zero to the INSERTNODE function and then deleting the node, however, as you will lose all of the active nodes. When you lose a node, it means that your list management functions (functions for adding, deleting, searching, etc.) will not be able to find that node. Lost nodes should never occur if the proper procedures are used to keep track of active and inactive nodes. However, careless programming can easily cause a node to get lost, as explained earlier.

The final step is to create a function to free, or delete, an active node and assign it to the inactive node list. The delete function I have outlined here doesn't allow you to delete the first item in your linked list, but you can easily modify it to do so. The function should take one parameter, a "pointer" to the node above the node to delete, named POS. The function need not return a value, however, it would be convenient to return a "pointer" to the node that the node you deleted pointed to. We will call the function, for the purpose of this example, DELETENODE. The function will first create a variable named TEMP and set its value equal to the value of INACT. Next, it will assign the value of INACT to be equal to the value of NODE[POS].NEXT. Then it will then assign the value of NODE[POS].NEXT to be equal to the value of NODE[NODE[POS].NEXT].NEXT. Finally, the function will assign the value of NODE[NODE[POS].NEXT].NEXT to be equal to TEMP.

When explicitly implementing a linked list I would also like to suggest adding a variable to keep track of the first node in your list. This way you will always know where to find the first node in your linked list, even if you delete the first node. You will find it convenient to have this piece of information on hand when writing a function to search the list.

Implicitly implementing a linked list

Implicitly implementing a linked list involves the use of pointers. A pointer, as defined earlier, is simply a variable that stores the memory address where a particular variable is stored. In order to implicitly implement a linked list, your programming language must support the use of pointers.

You need to define two types to use the "pointer implementation" of linked lists, one pointer type and one record type. We will create a pointer type named PTYPE that stores pointers to NODETYPE type variables and a record type named NODETYPE. NODETYPE will be defined the same way in this example as it was in the previous example.

Once these types are defined, you will create a pointer variable of our PTYPE type. We will name this variable P. When we are referring to the variable P by its value we will represent it as simply P. When we are referring to the node at the address that the variable P is pointing to we will represent it as &P. For example, if we want to reference the DATA field of a node in our linked list we would use &P.DATA. When we assign the pointer to the next node in out linked list we would use P = &P.NEXT.

For convenience, I will create a variable of our PTYPE type named FP to keep track of the first node in our list. FP will be equal to the memory address of the first node that we create. If we delete the first node in our list, FP will be reassigned to the node that the first item pointed to in its NEXT field before we deleted it.

Adding a new node is very simple, and can be done in one or two steps. Adding the new node to our linked list takes a few more steps. It is a good idea to add the new node to the linked list at the same time you create a new node as a simple coding error could cause a node to be lost. A lost node in an implicitly implemented linked list is lost forever, and the memory that is allocated for that node stays allocated until the program terminates. This type of unnecessary memory usage is called a memory leak. A memory leak occurs when memory is allocated for use, but not deallocated when it is no longer needed. Deallocation frees that memory space for use later. (Note, for future reference, that the process of deallocating memory that you no longer need is sometimes called garbage collection.)

Any language that supports pointers should also support dynamic memory allocation and deallocation. The names of the functions that different programming languages give to dynamic memory allocation are quite eclectic. The Pascal programming language uses the commands New and Dispose, the C programming language uses malloc and dealloc, and the C++ language include the functions new and delete to perform these operations. For the purposes of this example, we will name our commands New and Delete.

Our New function will work by accepting a pointer of the type that points to the type we desire to create as a parameter and returning a memory address. The function will allocate enough memory to store the type that our pointer is defined to point to. For example, to assign our pointer P to point to a new node, we would type "P=New(P)" (This will also allocate enough memory to store one instance of the NODETYPE type).

Our Delete function will work by simply accepting a pointer to a memory address as a parameter. It will not return any data, so no assignment is necessary. So to deallocate the memory that a node at memory location P occupies, we would type "Delete(P)".

So far we have created a pointer, but at present we don't have it pointing to a record in memory. Of course, in order to assign our pointer to a record, we must first create a record for it to point to. We will do this by using our New function and assigning the functions output to the pointer P. So we would type "P=New(P)". Now we have allocated enough space to store 1 node in memory and assigned our pointer P to the new node. Because this is the first node in our linked list, we will assign the pointer FP to point to it. We will do this by typing "FP=P".

Now that we have our node, we need to assign data to it. We can reference our node with the pointer that currently points to it. We will add the letter A to the DATA field or our linked list in this manner: &P.DATA="A". (The letter A is enclosed in quotes to show that we are not referring to a variable name A, but the literal character A.) We will also assign the NEXT field of our record a null value to show that it is the last node in our linked list by typing "&P.NEXT=null". We have now created a linked list with one node.

If we wanted to remove this node we could do so with our Delete function. Simply entering "Delete(P)" would deallocate the structure in memory that P points to.

Notes on List Management

For our convenience, we would want to create functions to make our list management easier. A set of standard list management functions will make working with linked lists easier. If the functions are designed properly, you will be able to use them in any program that you write (in the language they were implemented, of course) that use linked lists. This type of code reuse is common, and often encouraged. For example, an implementation of the C programming language will come with a standard library (written in the C language) of common functions. When you are writing your program in C, you use this standard library almost unconsciously. This standard library was designed in order to keep programmers from rewriting common functions each time they need to use them. These functions include functions for reading and writing files, displaying data on the screen, and receiving input from the user.

A list of linked list management functions we would implement should include:

Create   A function that creates a linked list with one node.

CheckEmpty   A function that checks to see if our linked list contains no nodes.

Insert   A function that inserts a node into a list after a specified node.

Remove	A function that removes a node after a specified node.
InsertLast	A function that inserts an item at the end of our list.
Search	A function that we can use to search our list.

You can design other functions as well, depending on how you would personally want to manage a linked list.

You're probably wondering how a search function in a linked list would work. The best way, unfortunately, to search a linked list, is by implementing a linear search. The linear search would operate by checking the first node, then reassigning the pointer to the NEXT field of that node, checking the new node and continuing to reassign the pointer until the data is located or a null is encountered in the NEXT field.

An example of a linear search function that searches for the letter Z:

1 Set our pointer P to be equal to FP
2 Check to see if &P.DATA is equal to "Z" if so then goto step 6
3 Set P equal to &P.NEXT
4 Check to see if P is equal to null if so then goto step 6
5 Goto step 2
6 Have the function return P

The function above will return the address of the pointer if the data is found, otherwise it will return null.

Modifications to our basic structure

Sometimes it is convenient to make a data structure more complex in order to simplify the use of our structure. For this reason, I will list some common modifications to the linked list that you may find useful. These modifications are not necessary, but could save you some trouble when using a linked list in certain applications.

Header nodes

Sometimes it is convenient to have a header node, or dummy node, as the first node in your linked list. The node will not actually be used, but will constantly point to the first real node in the list. This means that an empty list will still have one node. Using a header node can also allow us a few advantages. We could rewrite our routines so that we always use a pointer to the previous node to reference the actual node. This way, when we write our Remove function we can pretend that we are sending a pointer to the actual node to delete even though we are really sending a pointer to the previous node. The routine that receives the pointer will have to be coded with the understanding that it is receiving a pointer to the previous node, however.

Making your list circular

A circular list is simple to create, but slightly more difficult to maintain. A circularly linked list has no actual end, but instead the last item links to the first item (instead of being null) creating a circular link. If you're using a linear search, you must know how many items are in your list, or the location of the last node, to avoid looping through it forever. It is also handy to keep track of the locations of the first, last, and next to last nodes in the list for maintenance purposes (i.e. if you delete the first node and don't modify the last node, your chain will be broken and the last node will point to a memory location that doesn't contain a node).

Having a circular list is quite convenient for many operations as you can reach every node from your current node (if you transverse your list long enough, you will eventually find the first node). You also avoid have to check for a null NEXT field as none of the NEXT fields will be null. This can save a lot of trouble if you tend to forget to check for a null NEXT field.

Doubling the links in your list

From the examples earlier in this chapter, you can see how convenient it would be to be able to transverse the list backward. That is, if each node had a link to the node above it. Adding such a link creates what is called a doubly linked list. A doubly linked list naturally uses more memory, but can simplify many operations. For example, the technique mentioned above to simplify removing nodes can be replaced in a doubly linked list with a routine that accepts an actual pointer to the node to be deleted because the node above the node to be deleted can be identified by the link in the node to be deleted. This will also allow you to write an "insert above" function that will insert a node above a specified node. This technique naturally makes maintaining your list more complex, but simplifies its use dramatically.

Chapter 6 Exercises

1) What does a linked list emulate?

2) What is the least number of fields a list can contain?

3) What makes a linked list "Doubly linked"?

4) Describe pointers and their use in a linked list.

5) The first node in a linked list is called the _____ and the last node in a linked list is called the _____.

6) What does the null pointer usually indicate?

7) The null pointer is sometimes referred to as _____.

Answer the following questions as being true or false:

8) The data items in a linked list directly reflect their respective order in memory.

9) A pointer is a variable that contains the actual address of a data item in memory.

10) Individual nodes in a linked list can be accessed randomly.

Answer the following question to the best of your ability:

11) Cite at least two advantages a linked list has over arrays.

12) Cite at least two advantages arrays have over linked lists.

13) Describe the linear implementation of a linked list.

14) Describe two ways to represent a linked list in memory.

13) What two things must be defined to implicitly implement a linked list.

14) You can transverse a linked list both forward and backward if the list is _____.

15) Describe a circularly linked list.

7

Stacks

A stack is another abstract data type that you will see used in many places. In fact, stacks are very important when writing a program in a computer's assembly language (the human-readable form of machine code). Stacks are a very simple data structure with infinite usefulness. A stack operates like a list, but we only concern ourselves with the last item added to the list. This is called the top of the stack. When an item is removed, the top of the stack is the item that was added before the recently removed item.

Here is an example:

If we add items A, B, C, D to the stack in their respective orders, our stack would look like (from top to bottom):

> D ← D is at the top of the stack
> C
> B
> A

Anytime we remove an item, we are removing the item at the top of the stack. Our stack would look like:

C ← C is at the top of the stack
B
A

If we were to add another item to the stack, say item E, our stack would look like:

E ← E is at the top of the stack
C
B
A

Because of the way a stack operates, it is sometimes referred to as a LIFO structure (Last In, First Out) meaning that the last item added to the stack is the first item to be removed.

There are four common functions that you should define to operate on your stack. The first two are commonly seen in a computer's machine language.

Pop—the pop function (sometimes abbreviated as U for unstack) removes the topmost item from the stack, and returns its value

Push—the push function (sometimes abbreviated as S for stack) adds an item to the stack. If your stack has a fixed size, such as a stack implemented with an array, you need to make sure that there is room in your stack for the item to be added. If you attempt to add an item to a full stack you will induce a "stack overflow".

Peek—the peek function is used to return the topmost item in the stack without removing the item from the stack.

Empty—the empty function simply checks to see if the stack is empty and returns true or false depending on the results. This function is used to avoid certain errors associated with empty stacks. For example, if you tried to Pop an item off an empty stack, a stack underflow would be induced. The Pop function should call the empty function to determine if the stack is empty or not before attempting to remove and return the topmost item.

A stack can be used to reorder a stream of input data. Let's say that we want to reverse the order of a stream of characters that the user entered from the keyboard to display them on the screen. If the user entered the letters: A, B, C, D, and E we could push all of the letters onto the stack:

E ← Top of the stack
D
C
B
A

and pop them off them off one-by-one to display them on the screen.

The output would be: E D C B A

We could also reorder the input stream in a different way. Lets say that we received a coded message from a friend that we want to decode. Because your friend is your friend, we know that the message is encoded by simply reversing every pair of letters. Therefore, if the message was BADC, then the decoded message would be ABCD. We could use a stack to decode the message. Here is an example (remember that S is an abbreviation for Push, and U is an abbreviation for Pop):

We will enter the coded message at the keyboard (our input stream):

A I H M R E ! E

We will then push each letter pair onto the stack and immediately pop them off.

(We will show the stack, for this example, as a line of characters instead of a column for this example. The line will be order from bottom to top)

Stack operations: S, S, U, U, S, S, U, U, S, S, U, U, S, S, U, U

Stack state	Operation	Output
A	S	
A I	S	
A	U	I
	U	I A
H	S	I A

H M	S	I A
H	U	I A M
	U	I A M H
R	S	I A M H
R E	S	I A M H
R	U	I A M H E
	U	I A M H E R
!	S	I A M H E R
! E	S	I A M H E R
!	U	I A M H E R E
	U	I A M H E R E !

Given a stream of input characters and a list of operations to perform we could order our input stream in a number of different ways.

Given an input stream of: A B C D E
Performing the operations: S S S S S U U U U U
Our output stream would be: E D C B A

Given an input stream of: A B C D E
Performing the operations: S S U S U U S S U U
Our output stream would be: B C A E D

Or we could avoid changing the order at all:

Given an input stream of: A B C D E
Performing the operations: S U S U S U S U S U
Our output stream would be A B C D E

This reordering property has its limitations, however. Given an input stream of A B C D E we could never output E A B C D no matter what stream of operations we perform on our input stream.

This reordering property of stacks can allow us to store information that needs to be recalled in a certain order. This can be useful in several different places, including recursive algorithms and even during a program's execution. For example, when your program calls a function, the location from which it is called is pushed onto a stack. If that function in turn calls a function, its calling location is also pushed onto the stack. Because the location that each call was made needs to be known in order to return to the proper location when each function terminates in order, a stack makes an excellent structure for storing this information.

Implementing a stack using arrays

The simplest way to implement a stack is to use an array. Although using an array to implement a stack limits the amount of stack space (items that can be held in the stack), it is nonetheless a quick and easy way to implement a stack.

A stack requires two parts, a stack pointer and the list of items itself. The stack pointer simply identifies our current location in the stack. The list can be implemented as an array or as a linked list, as we will soon see.

There are several different ways that you can implement a stack using arrays. One way would be to declare your array and stack pointer as separate variables and passing each to your functions. The other way is to create a record type that contains the stack pointer and an array as fields. This is usually the preferred method, but we will use the first method mentioned for simplicity.

We will begin by creating an array of integers named ST of length 5. It's a very short stack, but it will be large enough to contain the amount of data for the example. Keep in mind that an array is indexed starting at 0, so that an array of 5 elements is numbered 0 to 4.

We will continue by creating an integer named SP to use as our stack pointer. However, before we initialize the stack pointer, we have a decision to make. Do we use the stack pointer to point to the last item added, or the next available location in the array?

It is natural to initialize a variable to zero (0). Unfortunately, initializing our stack pointer to zero in this case would mean that we are using the stack pointer to point to the location in the array that is to be populated next. I have found that this method is unintuitive, and can lead to confusion when implementing the different functions used to manipulate the stack. Some people prefer this method as they can use an unsigned integer (a number that uses the sign bit as part of the mantissa) and can therefore index more array elements. However, if your array contains fewer elements than can be indexed by a signed integer, the advantage is lost.

For our purposes, we will initialize the stack pointer to negative one (-1). This will allow us to use our stack pointer to point to the actual location of the item at the top of the stack. I personally prefer this method, and we will use it in our example. I have found that having the stack pointer point to an actual data item, my stack manipulation functions were easier to write, and easier to debug. It doesn't seem to matter one way or another which method you choose, but I have a particular preference for this method. Your preferences may differ, however.

The next step would be to create each of our routines. We will write the Empty function first, as it is a very simple function.

The Empty function is a value returning function (a function that returns a value) that accepts the stack pointer as a parameter and returns a Boolean value (true or false) dependent on whether or not the stack is empty (True for empty, False if otherwise). Because we use the stack pointer to point to the last item added to our stack, we need only check to see if SP is greater than negative one. A pseudocode example would be:

> 1) If SP is greater than -1 then return False
> 2) return True

I have shortened the form of pseudocode I have been using in this book significantly (more than usual) for this example. As the need to understand more about how programs operate becomes more important, I will make the pseudocode examples less verbose. For this example, however, I have also decided to show you how we can use one condition to test for two conditions. Because returning a value implies that the function ends, I decided that the algorithm need not be anymore complicated than the two lines I have composed. Also, because the function we are using returns a Boolean value, I can assume that if the function doesn't return false, then it must return true and vice versa. You can insert the word "otherwise" between lines 1 and 2 so that the algorithm reads "If SP >= -1 then return False, otherwise, return True". This should clarify the above example.

The next function that we will create is the Push function. This function, as you recall, will "push" an item onto the stack. (Note: We don't have a facility in place to check to see if the stack is full, however, for this example we will assume that our stack will always be a maximum of 5 items in length.) The pop function will accept our stack pointer (SP), our array (ST), and the item to be added (ITEM) as parameters, and return a Boolean value to determine if the push operation was successful. This function will also increment our stack pointer by one and assign the value of ITEM to the new array index that SP points to. We will assume, for this example, that the function will modify the values of the parameters we pass it. Our pseudocode example would be:

1) If SP is less than 4 then do the following:

1A) set SP equal to SP + 1
1B) set ST[SP] equal to ITEM
1C) return true

2) return false

This function is just as simple as the one before it. As I mentioned before, stack manipulation functions using arrays are incredibly simple to implement.

The next function we will cover is, naturally, the Pop function. The pop function simply removes an item from the stack and returns its value. There are, however, a few questions that must be considered before implementing this particular function. First, as a function can return a value of only 1 type, how do we return an error (if a pop function fails) to the user. We could have the function return true or false (for consistency) and return the value of the array element in a parameter passed to the function, but this over-complicates its use. We could also just return the value of the array element and use a special value to determine if the pop function fails, but then we would be limiting the type of information we could store in the stack and the function would be more complicated than necessary. Another way, and I'm sure you've thought of many more, would be to ignore the problem, and just return the value that was "popped" from the stack.

Ignoring the problem may seem like a bad idea at first, but consider the complications involved in checking every single time you call a pop or push function to see if it fails. Imagine checking every single function that you use in your program to determine if that function fails, and then handling that failure. It would be an absolute mess. Just about every compiler today will automatically generate code to handle program errors that are produced at runtime. For simple functions like the ones listed here, it is usually best to let the compiler do the dirty work for you. For example, if we were to remove the code in our push function that returns the Boolean value, and an error occurred when the program was running, the program would simply generate a "subscript out of range" error, meaning that we attempted to address an array element that is outside the bounds of our array. We will let our pop function do the same. Although if you're really concerned about returning an error, you can call the empty function before you call the pop function to be sure that there is data in the stack.

The pop function will accept 2 parameters, our stack pointer (SP) and our array (ST) and return the value of the item at the locate the stack pointer points to. This function will also decrement the stack pointer by one, logically removing the topmost item. A pseudocode example would be:

1) set SP = SP – 1
2) return ST[SP + 1]

Again this is a very simple function. You're probably wondering, at this point, why you would even bother to write functions to handle such simple operations. The answer is simple. Why write several lines of code over and over again when you could write them once and use just one line of code to implement them. Using functions this way saves memory, reduces the size of your program, and makes your code easier to read. I find that taking the time to write functions to perform common operations saves me time in writing my programs, and saves me time when debugging my programs.

The final function we will create will be the peek function. The peek function will simply return the item at the top of the stack without removing it. It is a very simple function as it only requires one line to implement. The function will simply accept our stack pointer (SP) and our array (ST) as parameters and return the topmost item in our stack. This function need only be one line long. Here is the pseudocode example:

1) return ST[SP]

You can see that the function is simply a modification of the pop function that simply doesn't decrement the stack pointer. Because this function is only one line, you could probably just use this line (modified) instead of creating a function, but using a function will make your code easier to read.

Implementing a stack using linked lists

You can also implement a stack using a linked list. A linked list isn't bound by the same size constraints as an array. (Note that implementing a linked list using an array would remove this advantage, and make implementing a stack using a linked list pointless. So for this example we will assume that you are implementing a linked list using pointers.) A linked list can grow to fit the size of available memory before running out of stack space. However, when removing the topmost item in the stack, great care must be given to ensure that the memory that the item was using is deallocated. If you "pop" an item off the stack without deallocating its storage space, you will create a memory leak.

There are several different ways to structure your linked list for use as a stack. You could create a doubly linked list, and use the last item in the list as the top of the stack. This method is very wasteful, however, it is easier to understand the structure. A better method would be to create a singly linked list, with each new node pointing backward to the node before it. This method is less wasteful and still easy to understand. The final, and preferred, method is to create a standard singularly linked list with each node pointing to the next node, and use the head node as the top of the stack. We will use this method for our example.

To begin we will define a structure to contain our data, and a pointer to the next item in the list. We will call our definition STTYPE and name our fields

DATA and NEXT. We will also define a pointer that points to an STTYPE item and name it SP. We will initialize SP to null to show that it currently points to no items, and that our stack is empty.

For the purposes of this example, we will assume that we can use the New and Delete functions from Chapter 6.

The first function we will create is the empty function. This function will accept SP as a parameter and return a Boolean value. It will function the same way as the empty function we created earlier. Here is the pseudocode example:

    1) If SP is equal to null then return True
    2) return False

The next function we will create is the Push function. This function will be slightly more complex than the push function we defined earlier, but it is still quite simple. Remember that we are using the head node as the top of the stack, so all items added will be added above the head node.

    1) create a pointer that points to an STTYPE type named TEMP
    2) set TEMP = SP
    3) set SP = New(SP)
    4) set SP.NEXT = TEMP

We create the TEMP pointer variable to store the location of the current head node so that we can point to it after the new head node is created.

The next function we will create is, naturally, the peek function. The operation is similar to the pop function we defined in the earlier example. The difference lies in the need for temporary storage of some data and memory cleanup that we previously allocated for the head node.

    1) create a pointer that points to an STTYPE type named TSP
    2) create a pointer that points to an STTYPE type named TD
    3) set TD = SP.DATA
    4) set TSP = SP
    5) set SP = SP.NEXT
    6) Delete(TSP)
    7) return TD

The pointer variable TSP is used to hold the value of the stack pointer so that we can delete the memory at that address. The pointer variable TD is used to hold the value of the DATA field that SP points to so that the function can return that data after its memory has been deleted.

The final function we will create is the peek function. The peek function is just as simple as the peek function form the earlier example. It can be performed in a single line, just as was done in the earlier example.

    1) return SP.DATA

You will notice that I made no attempt in the above examples to perform any sort of error checking before performing the operations. I've determined that taking the extra time to perform these checks would be superfluous, as I've already discussed the type of error checking that would be beneficial. In addition, the extra lines that are required to implement the checks would clutter the examples.

Chapter 7 Exercises

1) Describe how a stack operates.

2) List and describe four common functions that are used to perform operations on stacks.

3) What type of error results when you attempt to add an item to a full stack?

4) What type of error results when you attempt to remove an item from an empty stack?

5) What are some of the advantages that the reordering property of stacks provide?

6) What are the two part of a stack?

7) What are the two different ways to implement a stack using arrays?

8) What are the advantages that implementing a stack using a linked list has over implementing a stack using arrays?

9) What are the advantages that implementing a stack using arrays has over implementing a stack using linked lists?

10) Cite two ways to structure your linked list for use as a stack.

8

Queues

A queue is an abstract data type used to store items in a linear fashion, to be retrieved in the order that they were inserted. Queues are typically used to store items that need to be processed in a system where the items that need processed are created faster than the program can process them. (i.e. A queue may be used to store pages that need sent to the printer, because typically the pages can be generated faster than the printer can print them.) You can picture a queue as a group of people waiting in a line.

A queue is a FIFO type structure. Where a stack was a LIFO structure where the last item inserted was the first item retrieved (Last In First Out), in a queue the first item inserted is the first item retrieved (First In First Out).

Because intermediate data in a queue isn't accessible, there are only two locations in the queue that we need to concern ourselves with, the beginning of the queue, called the front, and the end of the queue, called the rear. An item will be retrieved (Dequeued) from the front and added (Enqueued) to the rear.

There are four functions we will create as an interface to our queue:

Enq (Enqueue)—This function will add an item to the end of our queue, and adjust the location of the end of the queue.

Deq (Dequeue)—This function will retrieve the item from the front of the queue, remove it, and adjust the location of the front of the queue.

Empty—This function will check to determine whether or not there is data waiting in our queue.

Peek—This function will return the data item at the front of our queue without removing it.

Only the first two are really necessary to interface with our queue, but you will find that the second two will be useful when using your queue in a program.

Implementing a queue

There are two ways to implement a queue in your program. The first way is to use an array to implement your queue, just as we were able to implement a linked list and stack using an array. The second way is to use a linked list (implemented with pointers) to implement your queue. The same limitation arises when using an array to implement your queue via an array as arises when implementing a stack via an array, the number of elements you can store is limited to the size of your array. This usually isn't a problem when you know how many items will be in your queue at any given time.

Using an array to implement a queue

When using an array to implement a queue, certain design issues become prevalent.

The first issue to consider is how data is to be stored in the queue when the underlying storage structure is an array. It is obvious that the data will be stored in a linear fashion, but the problem arises when an item is dequeued. There are two basic ways to solve this problem. The first and most obvious solution involves shifting every item in the queue up one position so that the front of the queue is always indexed at 0. This solution, however, causes some performance issues, as the time it takes to move the items in the queue up one location can be astronomical when there are many data items in the queue. The second solution, and the one we will be using, is to keep two variables that point to the front and rear of the queue. This complicates many of the calculations but increases the speed of your queue exceptionally. This solution also leads us to the second issue.

The second issue, now that it is decided we will use the second solution to the first issue, is how to properly fill our queue. Filling our queue is a very straightforward process of inserting items below each other in a linear fashion. The issue arises when the last item in the list is filled. Chances are that at this point, there will be several unused spaces in the array. To avoid running out of space, these extra spaces need to be filled, as data is available to fill them. To do this, after the last item is filled, the rear pointer must be moved to the top. In this way, we would be creating, in effect, a circular array. This causes several problems. After the rear pointer "wraps" to the first index, the rear pointer will be less than the front pointer (instead of the front pointer being less than the rear pointer). This makes calculating how many items are in the queue, and determining whether or not the list is empty or full extremely difficult. This leads us to the third and final issue.

The third issue that needs to be dealt with is how to test for an empty queue. There are two ways to solve this problem. The first, and simplest solution, is to simply store how many items are currently in the queue. The variable will be initialized as zero, and will be incremented or decremented depending on whether an item is enqueued or dequeued. The queue is empty if our variable is zero. Also, the number of elements in the queue is always available to us. The second solution is much more complicated. It involves using the values of the front and rear pointers to determine whether or not a queue is empty or full. We will cover this second solution in depth because it is a very interesting study that gives us insight to the type of problems encountered when building data structures.

Let's assume that our pointers point to the actual location of the first item in the queue and the last item in the queue. We will call our pointers F and R respectively. When we initialize them, both pointers will point to the first element in our array (element 0). For our illustration, we will place F and R underneath the array element that each represents. If an array element contains data, we will place an x in that element. An example would be:

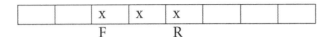

We will examine the state of our queue as items are enqueued and dequeued. This will allow us to understand the queues function more fully.

The queue starts empty, with the front and rear pointers pointing at the first element in the array as they are initialized to zero

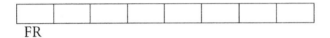

We will insert an item into the queue at the location of the rear pointer. In this way, the rear pointer will point to the next item to be filled. Because our array is circular, we will use a formula to calculate the location of the next item, instead of just adding one to our rear pointer.

$R = (R+1) \bmod L$

L in this case is the length of the array, in this case 8 (indexed 0 to 7). We use this formula because for any R less than L the value of R + 1 will be returned, and any R greater than L will return the remainder of the R / L plus 1, effectively pointing the next item to be filled at the top of the list. For example: if L = 8 and R = 7 then (R + 1) mod L which equals (7+1) mod 8 which equals 8 mod 8 which equals 0, the next item to be filled. The actual location of the rear item can't be calculated easily, but it should never be necessary. If we were to initialize R to -1 then the pointer would point to the actual location of the rear of the queue, but we would have to change our algorithms and some of our calculations.

Therefore, when we add an item to our queue the resulting queue would look like:

We will add several more items for the example:

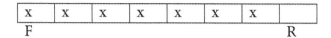

Now, if we were to fill the last space in our array R would equal F and we could use this condition to test to see if the queue were full. Unfortunately, this same condition occurs when our queue is empty. The solution is, of course, to waste a last space in our array so that the maximum number of items we can contain in our queue is L–1 as opposed to L. This way, when R is equal to F then our queue is empty.

We don't always waste the last space in our array, however. The wasted space is actually going to always be the space before F. When we add an item, we would simply check beforehand to be sure that R would not equal F after the operation. Here is an example:

If we were to take the current state of our queue and remove 2 items:

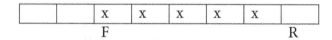

(Note that when updating the value of F when removing an item, we can use the same formula for calculating the new position of R. Swapping R for F, naturally, the formula for calculating the new value of F would be: F = (F +1) mod L)

Now we will add 2 items to our queue:

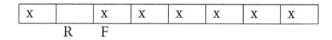

We can add no more items, because (R+1) mod L = F meaning that the queue is full.

We will not perform a similar check when removing items from our queue, as doing so would prevent the last item in our queue from being dequeued.

If we were to remove six items from our queue:

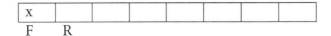

Checking to see if R = (F+1) mod L would prevent the operation from being performed, as the statement would evaluate to true in this case. Instead, we will not perform the check and thus we will be able to remove the item.

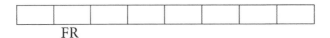

Now we have an empty queue. We can determine if our queue is empty by checking to see if F is equal to R.

Coding the operations

To give you a better understanding of queue implementation, I will give pseudocode examples of the Enq (Enqueue) and Deq (Dequeue) functions.

A pseudocode example of the Enq (Enqueue) function:

(Note that this function will accept the front and rear pointers (F and R), the length of the array (L), the array itself (Q), and the data to add (DATA) as parameters. Also, note that you could minimize the number of parameters by creating a record that holds F, R, L, and Q and simply passing the structure and DATA. We have kept each item separate to simplify the examples.)

1 if (R+1) mod L = F then goto step 5
2 set R = (R+1) mod L
3 set Q[R] = DATA
4 end function
5 display "overflow" on the screen
6 end function

A pseudocode example of the Deq (Dequeue) function:

(Note that this function will accept the front and rear pointers (F and R), the length of the array (L), and the array itself (Q) as parameters, and will return the value of the item that is dequeued.)

1 if F = R then goto step 7
2 create a variable called TEMP
3 set TEMP = Q[F]
4 set Q[F] = null
5 set F = (F+1) mod L
6 return TEMP
7 display "underflow" on the screen
8 end function

Implementing a queue with a linked list

Implementing a queue with a linked list is surprisingly simpler than implementing a queue with an array. Because there are no size constraints (except available memory) to consider when implementing the queue, no considerations need to be made to insure that previously used space is reused.

We will need to create a record type for our linked list that will contain a pointer to our next node and at least one field to contain the data. We will name the fields NEXT and DATA respectively. We will also create a pointer type that will point to an instance of our record type.

In this implementation two pointers are used, one to keep track of the head node which will represent the front of the queue and one to keep track of the tail node that will represent the rear of the queue. We will name the pointers F and R respectively.

Because of the nature of linked lists, when we create either the Enq (Enqueue) function or the Deq (Dequeue) function, only one of our pointers (either F or R) need to be passed. I will cover the implementation of both functions through pseudocode examples:

Coding the Operations

The Enqueue Function:
   (This function will accept 2 parameters, a pointer to the rear (tail node) of the queue named R and the data that is to be added to the queue named D. This function will not return a value)

```
1 create a pointer named T
2 set T = R
3 set R = New(R)
4 set T.NEXT = R
5 set R.DATA = D
6 set R.NEXT = null
7 end function
```

Notice that when we add the node to the bottom of the list, we save the location of the old tail node in T, then use T to set the old tail node to point to the new tail node. Review the chapter on linked lists for a more through explanation.

The Dequeue Function:

(This function only needs to accept one parameter, a pointer to the front (head node) of the queue named F. This function will also return a value.)

```
1 create a pointer named T
2 create a variable named TD
3 set T = F
4 set TD = F.DATA
5 set F = F.NEXT
6 Delete(T)
7 return TD
```

The pointer T is used to store the location of the old head node after it has been reassigned to the next node in the list. The variable TD is used to hold the DATA portion of the old head node so that it can be returned by the function after its memory space has been freed by the Delete function. Again, if any of the operations are not clear, please review the chapter on linked lists.

Chapter 8 Exercises

1) Define a queue

2) Does a queue allow random access to its elements?

3) List four functions that are commonly used to operate on queues.

4) Cite two ways to implement a queue in your program.

5) Describe a problem associated with an array implementation of a queue and its solution.

6) What advantages does a linked list implementation of a queue have over an array implementation?

7) Describe the process of retrieving an item from a queue in either an array or linked list implementation.

8) Describe the process of inserting an item into a queue in either an array or linked list implementation.

9) Describe a situation where a queue would be useful.

10) What are some of the disadvantages of implementing a queue via a linked list?

0-595-24039-9

www.ingramcontent.com/pod-product-compliance
Lightning Source LLC
Chambersburg PA
CBHW082110070326
40689CB00052B/4470